English
Historical Documents

ANDREW PRESCOTT

The British Library

© 1988 The British Library Board

Published by
The British Library,
Great Russell Street
London WC1B 3DG

and 27 South Main Street,
Wolfboro, New Hampshire
03894-2069

British Library Cataloguing in Publication
Data

English historical documents.
  1. Great Britain. History
  I. Prescott, Andrew
  941

ISBN 0-7123-0158-5

Designed by Roger Davies
Typeset in Monophoto Ehrhardt by August
Filmsetting, Haydock, St Helens
Origination by York House Graphics,
Hanwell
Printed in England by Jolly and Barber Ltd,
Rugby

Inside front cover: Letter from
Queen Elizabeth I to Thomas
Randolph, her agent in Scotland, 2
February 1566. From the papers of
William Cecil, Lord Burghley,
Elizabeth's chief minister for most
of her reign, purchased by the
British Library in 1807.
[Lansdowne MS.8, f.95]

Title page: Impression of the
second great seal of Elizabeth I,
designed by Nicholas Hilliard and
used from 1586 to 1603.
[Detached Seal, XXXVI.19]

This page and opposite page: Initials
from an early 16th-century register
of deeds and other documents of
Waltham Abbey in Essex.
[Harley MS 3739, ff. 12v, 65, 90]

Inside back cover: Draft of British
ultimatum to the German
government following the invasion
of Poland, September 1939. From

the papers of Lord Harvey of
Tasburgh (1893–1968), private
secretary to the foreign secretary,
Lord Halifax.
[Add. MS 56401, f.161]

Front cover: Grant by King James
I to Sir John Hollis of the title of
Baron Haughton of Haughton, 9
July 1616. The initial contains a
stylised portrait of the king and
the illuminated borders
incorporate the royal arms.
[Add. Charter 32975]

Back cover: Letter dated 4 August
1854 from Queen Victoria (reigned
1837–1901) to Lord Aberdeen, the
prime minister at that time. The
elaborate letterhead shows
Osborne House on the Isle of
Wight, designed by Victoria's
husband, Prince Albert and
completed in 1851.
[Add. MS 43049, f.233]

ACKNOWLEDGEMENTS
The help of Peter Barber, David
Blake, James Elliot, Frances
Harris, Elaine Paintin, Arthur
Searle, Rachel Stockdale, Barry
Taylor, Christine Thomas and
Christopher Wright in the
preparation of this volume is
gratefully acknowledged.

The British Library has made
every effort to trace copyright
holders of the items illustrated and
is grateful for permission to
reproduce the following: 84,
courtesy of News International;
inside back cover illustration,
courtesy of The Honourable John
Harvey.

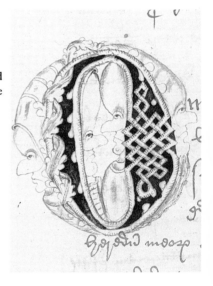

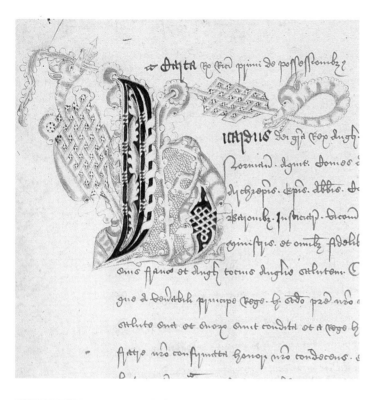

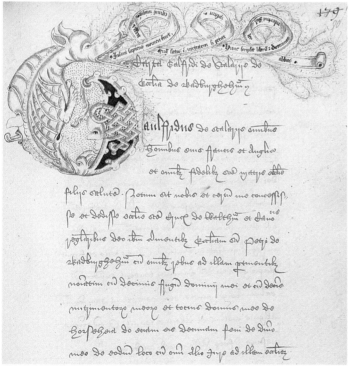

Contents

1 A charter of King Stephen. This charter was issued by King Stephen (reigned 1135–54) in late 1146 or early 1147, at the height of his struggle for the English throne with his cousin, the Empress Matilda. It informs all archbishops, bishops, abbots, earls, justices and others that Stephen had granted to Reading Abbey the manor of Blewbury in Berkshire. The seal is Stephen's second great seal, used by him from 1139 to the end of his reign. Shortly afterwards, the monks of Reading apparently took the precaution of obtaining a separate grant of this land from Matilda.

[Add. Charter 19581.]

Introduction

Documents are as important to historians as physical objects are to archaeologists. They are the material from which they attempt to reconstruct the past. Many historical documents may at first sight seem more forbidding and less evocative than the objects recovered by archaeologists. Their language may be an unfamiliar one and they may be written in an apparently indecipherable scrawl. Nevertheless, they contain direct evidence of the way people thought and felt in the past and can give a vivid picture of their lives and personalities. Moreover, documents often played a central part in major events and through their historical associations alone can create a sense of intimate contact with the past.

This does not of course mean that historians only rely on written sources. All survivals from the past are grist to the historian's mill and historians are increasingly making use of non-documentary evidence. The study of the landscape, for example, can reveal a great deal about earlier forms of economic organisation. Historians studying the early medieval period make extensive use of place-names and numismatic evidence in attempting to determine settlement patterns. Nevertheless, the vast majority of the sources currently used by historians are still of the traditional written kind.

This book contains a selection of documents from the British Library relating to English history and attempts to illustrate some of the many forms historical documents take. The term 'historical documents' does not relate to any special category of manuscript or printed book, but is simply a convenient way of referring to all the various types of manuscript and printed sources used by historians. These range from medieval chronicles, accounts and charters to modern pamphlets, newspapers and letters. Indeed, any written material from the past can be an interesting historical source. Novels, for example, often contain useful information about contemporary social conditions. Historians sometimes make a distinction between 'documentary' sources like administrative records and 'literary' sources such as contemporary narratives, which might seem to suggest that a narrower definition of historical documents is possible, but this is not the case, since many sources such as letters can be both 'documentary' and 'literary' in character.

To assist them in the use of documents, historians have to acquire a number of special skills. The most important of these is a critical sense. The reliability of each document and its limitations as evidence have to be carefully appraised. An eye-witness account of a particular event may seem an unimpeachable source, but its author may have been biased or used hearsay to add colourful details to his description. Similarly, the information in administrative documents reflects the purpose for which they were compiled and in using them as evidence it is necessary to understand something of the system which generated them. Occasionally historians may even encounter forged documents. The forging of charters to support land claims was commonplace in the middle ages, while the recent controversy over the 'Hitler diaries' illustrates the pitfalls which await unwary historians of more recent periods.

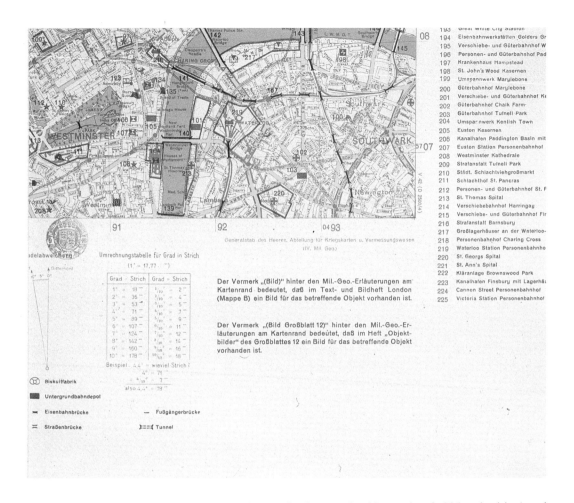

Some knowledge of palaeography (the study of old handwriting) and diplomatic (the analysis of the form of documents) is also vital to historians. The forms of letters in medieval and early modern handwriting were often completely different to those used today and extensive use was made of abbreviations, so that considerable training is necessary to read documents of those periods. It can even be difficult to read more modern documents fluently. Palaeography can also sometimes be a useful aid in dating documents. Diplomatic is helpful in understanding the structure and phraseology of administrative and legal documents and in distinguishing common form from significant information.

Historians also need to be aware of the various methods of expressing dates used at different times. Even when dates are given in a modern form, they can be misleading. Until 1752 the new year in England was considered to begin on 25 March, so that a document dated 23 March 1601 would according to modern reckoning have been written in 1602. This is not the only possible source of confusion. Because the calendar used in the middle ages was not accurately related to the earth's orbit, by the 16th century it was about ten days behind astronomical time. Pope Gregory XIII ordered that this should be corrected by shortening the year 1582 and altering the frequency of leap years. This edict was not, however, recognised by non-catholic countries including England, which continued to use the old calendar, so that various dates were assigned to the same day in different parts of Europe. England did not adopt the new calendar until 1752.

Despite the fact that they require such a variety of documentary skills, historians possess no distinctive intellectual techniques to help them in using the information in documents to resolve the controversies of the past, but rely chiefly on their common sense and general intelligence. This reflects the fact that the modern approach to the study of history is an amalgam of an antiquarian tradition which stressed the study of documentary minutiae and the more general literary approach of historians such as Gibbon and Macaulay. History is far from being an exact science. The conclusions of historians vary widely and they have different points of view about every conceivable issue from the effects of the Norman conquest to the causes of the second world war. The study of history remains in many ways more of a literary activity than a science. Indeed, the methodology of historians differs little from that of journalists. Historians, however, have two great advantages over journalists. They usually have more time in which to carry out their researches and they have access to a much wider range of documents relating to the events they are investigating.

Historians of England are fortunate in the wealth of documentation available to them. The national archives, kept at the Public Record Office, are amongst the oldest and most complete in the world. Enormous numbers of local records are available through the network of county record offices, while there are magnificent collections of other material in such great libraries as the Bodleian in Oxford. Of these institutions, the British Library is remarkable not just for the size of its holdings but also for the range of different types of material it contains.

At the centre of the Library's holdings of historical documents are the Manuscript Collections, which include not only 'private' documents such as personal letters but also many national and local records of a more 'official' character. The Library also houses an important section of the national archives, the India Office Records. It possesses the country's principal collections of newspapers and government publications. As one of the institutions in which a copy of every book published in Britain must be deposited in order to comply with copyright legislation, the Library also forms in effect an archive of modern British printed material. This is supplemented by an outstanding collection of books from earlier periods. The Library is not, however, just concerned with books in English. Its holdings of foreign literature are unparalleled in Britain and contain many documents from abroad relating to English history. The Library's special collections include the country's chief collection of maps, which contain a great deal of historical information, and the national archive of sound recordings, which are an increasingly important form of historical source.

2 A German bombing map. Historical documents assume many different forms. Maps are a very useful historical source. This is part of a map issued to German bomber crews in 1941 to help them identify targets in London. It is a copy of an English Ordnance Survey map on which have been printed special symbols showing the different types of building and other information. A German key is also provided. Amongst the buildings marked in the section illustrated here are the Houses of Parliament, Westminster and Waterloo bridges, St Thomas's Hospital and Bankside power station.

[Map Library, 1255. (2.)]

The middle ages

The act which ultimately had most influence on the formation of the British Library's collections of medieval material was the dissolution of the monasteries by Henry VIII (reigned 1509–1547). No effective measures were taken at this time to safeguard monastic libraries and archives. Although a number of manuscripts were taken from religious houses and added to the old Royal Library, now in the British Library, these represented only a tiny part of the great monastic collections of manuscripts, which were otherwise generally regarded as worthless and dispersed. By the end of the 16th century, the historical interest of this material had begun to be more widely appreciated and several antiquaries attempted to gather it together again in order to preserve it for posterity. The most successful of these collectors was Sir Robert Cotton (1571–1631), who procured for his library not only such treasures as two of the earliest manuscripts of Bede (3), a number of versions of the Anglo-Saxon chronicle (5) and two of the four surviving original texts of Magna Carta (12), but also numerous deeds, chronicles and monastic registers. Cotton's library was settled on the nation by his grandson in 1700, but, despite a disastrous fire in 1731 in which many manuscripts were destroyed, no special provision was made for its accommodation until 1753, when it became one of the foundation collections of the British Museum, passing to the British Library at the time of its creation in 1973.

Inevitably Cotton and his contemporaries missed many of the manuscripts taken from the monasteries and the opportunities available to later collectors are apparent from the activities of Robert and Edward Harley, 1st and 2nd Earls of Oxford, who in the first half of the 18th century acquired more than 7,000 manuscripts, including many important medieval items, which were purchased by the British Museum at the time of its foundation. A large number of the medieval manuscripts bought by successive Keepers of Manuscripts in the 19th century and incorporated in the series of Additional and Egerton Manuscripts were monastic in origin. Even today, the Library still regularly acquires, by purchase in salerooms such as those of Sotheby's and Christie's and through occasional generous donations, manuscripts which have remained in private hands since they were removed from monasteries more than 400 years ago.

The most important historical documents produced by monasteries were chronicles, which provide the basic narrative framework of medieval history and identify the chief issues of the period. The most common form of chronicle originated in the tradition of keeping annals. In order to establish the dates of moveable feasts in the Christian year, monasteries and churches possessed tables showing when Easter should be celebrated. Notes were often made on these tables of memorable events in a particular year. These annals began to be kept in separate books and the entries for each year became longer, eventually developing into elaborate narrative accounts of contemporary events. The sophisticated level of historical writing achieved by medieval chroniclers is apparent from the series of chronicles produced by various monks of St Albans between the 13th and 15th centuries, the most famous of which are the works of Matthew Paris

3 An early Bede manuscript. The Venerable Bede (died 735), a monk of Jarrow in Northumbria, was the first great English historical writer. The *History of the English Church and People*, his most famous work, tells the story of the conversion of the English people to Christianity and is the chief source of information about English history from the arrival of St Augustine in Kent in 597 until 731. This manuscript was produced in southern England in the second half of the 8th century and is one of the oldest surviving copies of his work.

[Cotton MS Tiberius C.II, f.5v]

(**13–15**). These contain detailed and well-informed accounts of political events, with vivid descriptions of the main protagonists, discussion of the causes and significance of particular incidents and transcripts of key documents, some of which have not survived elsewhere.

The writing of chronicles became a popular form of literary activity and other people apart from monks began to produce them. In the late 12th century, a number of chronicles were compiled by secular clerks with an administrative background such as Roger of Howden (**11**). These provide important insights into the major developments in the legal and administrative system taking place at this time. The reading of chronicles became a popular form of entertainment and in the 13th and 14th centuries chronicles in French compiled by laymen like Jean Froissart appeared, intended for a noble audience and full of colourful tales of chivalry and valour (**19**).

Chronicles were not the only form of historical document produced by monasteries. Saints' lives and other hagiographical collections, for example, can be useful historical sources, particularly when the saint in question was such a prominent figure as Thomas Becket (**10**). The church also played an important part in the development of legal and administrative documents. It started to receive gifts of land almost as soon as the conversion of England began in the 6th century. Land tenure was at this time regulated by unwritten custom, but the church was anxious that the grants it received should be recorded in writing. The collections of Anglo-Saxon charters, the chief source of information about early English society, in the British Library and elsewhere consist mostly of remnants of the archives built up by religious houses during this period. In order to protect their records against accident or theft, monasteries made copies of their deeds in registers known as cartularies, which are also a valuable historical source.

The church's example encouraged the use of written documents in royal government. The Anglo-Saxon kings had already developed by the 11th century an advanced administrative system. The efficiency of the governmental machinery inherited by William the Conqueror is apparent from the speed with which the detailed survey of England recorded in Domesday Book was carried out. William's successors built on these foundations and by the 13th century England possessed perhaps the most sophisticated and effective legal and administrative system in Europe. The structure and operation of this system is explained in treatises like that formerly attributed to Henry Bracton (**16, 17**). The central records of the government, which are the most important source for English medieval history after the chronicles, are mostly still preserved in the Public Record Office. A number of these records, however, have strayed from official custody and are found in other collections such as those of the British Library (**18**). Moreover, the Library also contains innumerable examples of documents sent by royal officials to various corporate bodies and private individuals, of which the letters publicising the text of Magna Carta are the most famous examples (**12**).

As the church and crown produced more and more documents, literacy

4 The earliest mention of King Arthur.

This passage from the *History of the Britons* by Nennius, a Welshman writing in the 9th century, contains the first ever literary reference to King Arthur. The 3rd to 6th lines shown here read (in Latin): 'Then Arthur, together with the Kings of Britons, fought against them [the invading Saxons] in those days; but he was the leader in battle'. Nennius then lists twelve battles fought by Arthur; Arthur was, he declares, 'victorious in all his campaigns'. This is the oldest known manuscript of Nennius and dates from the 10th century.

[Harley MS 3859, f.187]

became more common and the use of written records more widespread. The preparation of written records during the conveyancing of land became standard practice. The pioneer in the use of written documents in estate administration was again the church and most of the Library's collection of manorial records, the basic source for English local history in the middle ages, is from monastic archives. The church's example was, however, followed by the laity and the Library also possesses many manorial records relating to estates held by laymen (**22**). As the inhabitants of towns became more autonomous, they also began to produce written records (**21**).

Most medieval documents are very stiff and formal. Lively circumstantial details and pen portraits of important personalities are generally only to be found in chronicles. Although personal letters survive, these are usually self-consciously literary productions written in high-flown language. During the 15th century, with the continued growth of lay literacy, informal letters in everyday English became more commonplace (**25, 26**). By the 16th century, letters such as these had become the chief form of historical document and have remained so to the present day.

inn to exanceastre. ⁊ þy geare healfdene norðan hymbra
land gedælde ⁊ ergende wæron ⁊ hira tilgende wæron.

her com se here to exanceastre fram werehā ⁊ þa metthe
micel mystonræ. ⁊ þær for wrað. cxx scypa æt swanewic.

⁊ þy cing ælfred æfter þam gehorsodan here mid fyrde rad
oþ exanceaster. ⁊ hi hindan ofridan ne mihte. ⁊ hi him gylas
sealdon ⁊ wærla ⁊ wrhe habban woldæ ⁊ micle aþas sworon
⁊ ða godne frið heoldon. ⁊ þa on hær fæste gefor se here on
myrcna land ⁊ hit gedældon sum ⁊ rum ceol wulfe sealdon.

her hine bestæl se here on midne winter ofer .xii. niht
to cyppanhamme ⁊ geridon wessexna land ⁊ þar gesæton
⁊ micel þæs folces ofer sæ adræfdon. ⁊ þær oþres þone mæstan
dæl hi geridon ⁊ þ folc hym to gebigde buton þam cininge
ælfrede. he lytle werede uneþelice æfter wudum for. ⁊ on
mor fæstenum. ⁊ þær ilcan wintres wær inwæres broðor
⁊ heafdenes on wessexna rice mid .xxiii. scypa ⁊ hine mon
þær ofsloh ⁊ dccc. manna mid him ⁊ .lx. manna hir heres.
⁊ þær wæs se guð fana genumen þe hi hrarenhetton.

⁊ nð þæs on eastron worhte ælfred cing lytle werede geweorc
æt æþelinga igge ⁊ of þam geweorce wæs winnende wið
þone here ⁊ rum up wætena se dæl se ðær nehst wæs. þa on
þære .vii. pucan ofer eastron he gerad to ecgbryhter stane
be eastan sealwuda ⁊ him comon þær ongen rum up wæte
ealle. ⁊ wilwæte ⁊ ham tun scir se dæl þe hire beheonan wæs.
⁊ hir gefægne wæron. ⁊ he for þæs embe ane niht of þam picū
to iglea. ⁊ ðæs eft embe ane niht to eðandune. ⁊ þær gefaht
wið ealne þone here ⁊ hine geflymde ⁊ him æfter rad

5 (*Left*): The *Anglo-Saxon Chronicle*.

The *Anglo-Saxon Chronicle*, probably begun at the command of King Alfred (reigned 871–99), was the first history of England in the English language. Six versions of the Chronicle, kept up to date at different monasteries, survive; four of these are in the British Library. Illustrated here is a page from a text probably copied at Abingdon Abbey in about 1046. The last paragraph describes the defeat of the Danes by King Alfred at Edington in Wiltshire in 878.

[Cotton MS Tiberius B.I, f.132]

6 A grant of King Canute.

Legal documents such as grants of land and wills provide extremely detailed information about Anglo-Saxon society. This is the record of a grant of land at Newnham in Nottinghamshire to the monk Ælfic by King Canute (reigned 1016–35) made between 1021 and 1023. The first part, which declares the terms o the grant, is in Latin, while the second section, in the smaller writing, describes in Old English the boundaries of the land. At the end is a list of witnesses. [Cotton MS Augustus II.24]

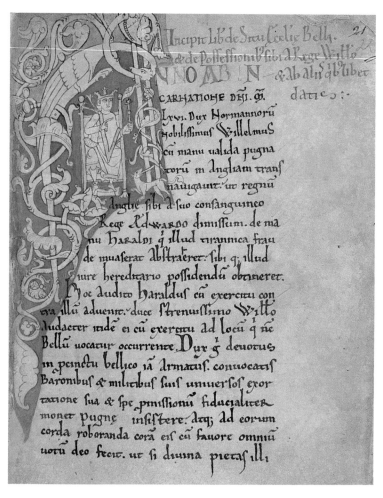

7 William the Conqueror. This picture of William I (reigned 1066–87) is from the unique manuscript of a 12th-century chronicle of Battle Abbey, which William founded on the site of the Battle of Hastings as an act of thanksgiving for his victory there in 1066. As was usual in the middle ages, the picture was not intended to be a realistic portrait.
[Cotton MS Domitian II, f.22]

8 The Conqueror's mark. These crosses were made by William the Conqueror, his wife Matilda and other nobles with their own hands to signify their approval of a grant of land in Suffolk and a house in London by Waleran, the son of Ranulf the moneyer, between 1072 and 1076. William's mark is in the middle of the top row and Matilda's is beside it on the left.
[Add. Charter 75503]

9 (*Right*): The making of Domesday Book. This record, known as the 'Inquest of the County of Cambridge', was compiled in the course of the elaborate survey of England made at the command of the Conqueror in 1086, the findings of which are summarised in Domesday Book. The Cambridge Inquest was based on notes taken during the hearings of the commissioners who made the survey and contains information omitted from Domesday Book. It is known only from this 12th-century transcript.
[Cotton MS Tiberius A.VI, f.71]

eidem tre semp iacuit. ⁊ uetra
Lun. nummos ⁊ consuetudines p
annu.

71 72

Stapleta
hund́

Hornincebrigge scira. In staple
hou hundr̃. iurauerunt homi
nes. scilicet Nicholaus de kenet.
⁊ hugo de heselinges. Wills de
cypeham. Warinus de saham.
Rob. de fordham. Ormar de bel
lingeha. Alanus de burunelle.
Aluric de sneilewelle. pcitus
uicecomes ⁊ omnes franci ⁊
angli.

In hoc hundreto nicholaus
tenet de will de uuarenne. p
iii. ⁊ dimid. se defendit t.r.e. ⁊
in p.ii. ⁊ dimidia. x. car. ibi. e. t.
v. in dominio. ⁊ v. uillanis.
vi. uillani. ⁊ i. pbr. ⁊ xii. serui.
⁊ molend. e. ibi. ⁊ ich reddit. pt
duab. c. pecunia in dominio.
vii. animal ociosa. ⁊ cccc. ⁊
iii. ix. oues. ⁊ porc. iiii. runcini.
Pastura ⁊ ad pecun. uille. In to
tis ualentiis. xii. lib. ⁊ qn recepit
xii. li. ⁊ t.r.e. xii. li. Hoc mane
riu tenuit hobillus teign regis
eduuardi. Et in hoc manerio
fuit qd sochemann Godric. ho
e. potuit dare sine licentia dni
sui tra sua. t.r.e. una uirgata

In hoc hundr̃. Ormar̃ de comite
Alano. Belmegesha. p. iii. h̄. ⁊
dimi. vi. c. se defendit t.r.e. ⁊ in
p.ii. h̄. ⁊ dimi. vi. c. i. e. tra. due
car. in dominio. ⁊ iii. uill. xr.
uill. ⁊ xvi. bor. vi. ser. ⁊ ii. molend.
unu molend. ii. sol. red. ⁊ aliud
motura: in dominio. Pratum
duab. c. Pastura ad pecun. uille
ii. animal. ociosa. lx. o. xx. porc.
ii. runc. In totis ualentiis ualet
lx. sol. ⁊ qn recepit. lx. sol. t.r.e.
c. sol. Hoc maniu tenuit Ormar̃
homo edluie. t.r.e. eaduuardi. potuit
dare cui uoluit. In hoc hundr̃
gaufridus de mandauilla. cypeha
x. h̄. tempe. r.e. ⁊ hec hide n defen
derunt se. in. p.v. h̄. Et uicecomes ipi
uicecommtatus fec has. x. h. defende
p.v. h̄. t.r.e. xvii. c. e. i tra. iii. in
dominio. ⁊ viii. uill. xxii. uillani.
xiii. bor. vi. serui. Pratum. iii. car.
Pastura ad pecunia uille. xiiii. an.
xx. porci. ccc. oues. xv. mun. iii. runc.
⁊ unu molend. de una piscina.
mille anguille ⁊ dimid. In totis
ualentiis. xx. lib. ⁊ qn recep. xvi. lib.
t.r.e. xii. lib. Hoc maniu tenuit

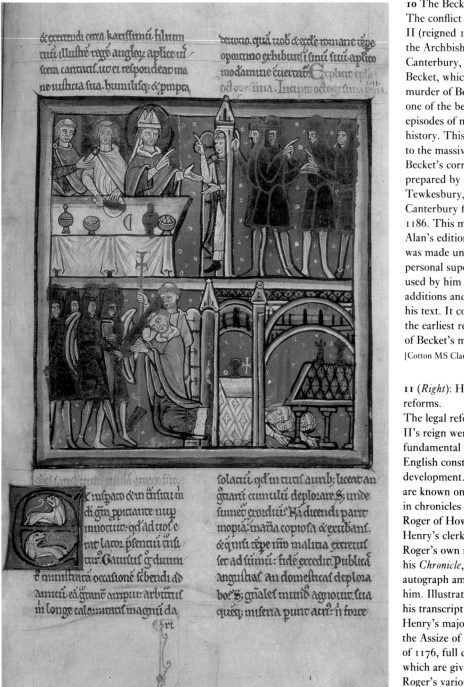

de exercendi circa karissimum filium tuum illustrem regem angloꝝ apostolice tui scera. cantuaris. uos et respondeam manone iusticia sua. humilisꝗ; & prompta

deuotio. quam uob̄ & eccle romane tempe oportuno exhibuint ī sinu suu aplico modamine cueruaꝶ Explicit epꝉa od̄ oꝯ sima. Incipit octogesima ꝓma.

obes sanct ...enī eiuda amico suo. K inspaco & in trīstitu ī di gꝶa ꝓpriante nup innouitur: qd̄ ad uoꝉ ē rat lator psentiū trīsitur. Gauisus ꝗ duum ē ministrata occasione scbendi ad amiciū eā gꝶaru amipit: arbitrui in longe calamitatis magnū da

solaciū qd̄ in titul auribꝰ; liceat an gꝶarū cumulii deplorare.S; unde sumeꝰ exordiū? Nā dicendi partū inopiā: mataa copiosa & exubant. & q̄ nisi tempe imo malicia exerceret ser ad sumū: fidē excedit. Publicā angustiat an domesticai deplora bo? S; gꝶales mundi agnouit sua queꝗ; miseria punt acui: ī foꝛce

10 The Becket letters.
The conflict between Henry II (reigned 1154–89) and the Archbishop of Canterbury, Thomas Becket, which led to the murder of Becket in 1170, is one of the best-documented episodes of medieval history. This is largely due to the massive collection of Becket's correspondence prepared by Alan of Tewkesbury, Prior of Canterbury from 1179 to 1186. This manuscript of Alan's edition of the letters was made under his personal supervision and used by him to record additions and corrections to his text. It contains one of the earliest representations of Becket's martyrdom.
[Cotton MS Claudius B.II, f.341]

11 (*Right*): Henry II's legal reforms.
The legal reforms of Henry II's reign were of fundamental importance in English constitutional development. Their texts are known only from copies in chronicles such as that of Roger of Howden, one of Henry's clerks. This is Roger's own manuscript of his *Chronicle*, incorporating autograph amendments by him. Illustrated is part of his transcript of one of Henry's major enactments, the Assize of Northampton of 1176, full details of which are given only in Roger's various writings.
[Royal MS 14.C.II, f.158]

iudicium curie sue de eis hñ
uoluerit sic de contemptoulx pcep
n̄ suo. | ⁊ ℞. ꝯ.
ystie inq̄rant de ex caetis. de
eccliis. de tris. de feminis. q̄ sr̄t
de donatione dn̄i regis. Item.
Balliui dn̄i regis respondē
ant ad scaccarium tam
de assiso redditu q̄m de omibz
pquisrtionibz suis q̄ faciunt in
ballīis suis exceptis ist q̄ pti
nent ad uicecomitatū. Item.
Iustrie inq̄rant de custodiis ca
stellorum ⁊ qui ⁊ q̄rtum ⁊ ubi
eas debeant ⁊ postea mandent
ꝯtro ex q̄ Item. dn̄o regi.
capit̄ uice comita t̄dat ad cu
stodiendum. ⁊ si uicecomes ab
sens furit. ducat ad pximū ca
stellanū ⁊ ipe illū custodiat
don̄ illū libꝰ uicecomiti. Item.
iustrie faciant querere p con
suetudinē tre illos qui d̄ regno
recesserunt. ⁊ n̄ redire uoluerit
infra tminū nōiatum ⁊ stare
ad rectum in curia dn̄i regis.
postea uthlagent̄. ⁊ nōia utla
gorz afferant ad pascha ⁊ ad
festum sc̄i michaelis ad scac
carium ⁊ ex in mittant̄ dn̄o
regi. Ad pdictum ū conciliū
apd horhamtun celebratū.
uenit Willms rex scottorz per
mandatū dn̄i regis ad duces

secum ricardum epm sc̄i an
dree. ⁊ Gocelinū epm de glas
cou. ⁊ Ricardū epm de dun
kelden. ⁊ xpianum epm de
candida casa. ⁊ andrea epm
de catenesse. ⁊ symonē de tou
ni epm de murewia. ⁊ Abbes
⁊ pores regni sui. Qui tū cora
dn̄o rege anglie conuenisset.
pcepit eis dn̄ rex ptide q̄m
ei debebant ⁊ p sacrm̄tū fideli
tatis q̄d ei fecerant. q̄d eand
subiectionē facient anglica
ne ecclie q̄m face debebant
⁊ solebant t̄pr regū anglie
pdecessorz suorz. Cui responde
runt q̄d ipi numq̄ subiectionē
fecarnt anglicane ecclie nec
face debent. Ad hoc autē res
pondit Rogus eboracensis ar
chiepc affirmans quod glas
cuenses epi ⁊ epi de candida
casa subiecti fuerant ebora
censi ecclie t̄pr archieporz p
decessorz suorz. ⁊ sup hoc pui
legia romanorz pontificum
sufficient̄ instructa. pmon
strauit. Ad quod Jocelinus
glasuensis epc respondit.
Glasuensis ecclia specialis
filia ⁊ Romane ecclie ⁊ ab
omi subiectione archiepor
sue eporz exempta. ⁊ n̄ ebo
racensis ecclia aliquo t̄pr do

12 (*Pages 18–19*): Magna Carta.
Magna Carta is widely regarded as the cornerstone of liberty in the English-speaking world, but it is in fact a series of detailed concessions on legal procedure and feudal rights wrung from an unwilling King John (reigned 1199–1216) by his noble opponents in 1215. Shown here is one of the letters sent throughout the kingdom by the royal chancery to publicise the terms of the grant. These letters contain the first authoritative text of Magna Carta. Four such letters have survived; two are in the British Library.
[Cotton MS Augustus II.106]

13, 14 (*This page*): Matthew Paris.
Matthew Paris (died 1259) was one of the most readable and prolific medieval chroniclers. In order both to stir the imagination and allow references to particular subjects to be found more easily, Matthew decorated his chronicles with drawings. The sketches on this page are from the autograph manuscript of Matthew's *History of the English*. The drawing on the right shows the Archbishop of Canterbury interceding with Henry III in 1234 on behalf of the Earl of Pembroke. The sketches shown below refer to two events in 1245, the start of work on the new Westminster Abbey and the general council of the church at Lyons.
[Royal MS 14.C.VII, f.122v, 138v]

15 (*Opposite*): The jewels of St Albans.
The *Book of Additions* was an appendix to Matthew's chief work, the *Greater Chronicle*, and contained copies of documents which could not be fitted into the main chronicle. Matthew also used the book for all kinds of rough notes, jottings and sketches. This is part of his illustrated description of the jewels in the treasury of St Albans Abbey.
[Cotton MS Nero D.I, f.146v]

prior de Walingeford deo 7 ecce sci Alban'
Casto aut continens eande gema 7 linon 7
ipe lapis ad maiore cancelam 7 secuta
tem eade aureo oculo cene'uigitur
prout in capite hui' capituli figurat'.
Ponderat aut ser denar' De Saphiro.

Hunc lapide p com'sum dni Nich.
videlicet saphiru fere rotundu
et coloris remissi dedit domin'
Nicholaus auris'ab de sco alba-
no oriundus; deo 7 ecce s. alb'. H gema
estq; fuit bi Admundi cant archiepi.
Postea uero Sci Robti fris ei'. Postea u
memorati dni Nicholai. In libo si'ede
castonis sbtilissime lite isculpuntur
nigellate. et erur cu crucifixo figurat'.
Ponderat aut ser den. De amulo Archidi.

Hunc Anulu co'tinente aconu iohis.
unu Saphiru orientale intensi
coloris dedit huic ecce dns Iohis
de Wmudha hui' ecce Archidiac'
Que de dono dni Rogi ecce h' pon's
optinuerat. In una q parte Anuli ad
memoria h' nois iohis p'petuandam;
isculpit 7 nigellat h lita I. ex alia uero.
O. Pondat aut noue den 7 ob. d anulo Ric.

Hunc Anulu co'tinentem Anima
Saphiru orientale coloris itensi
dedit dns Ric' cognome'to Animal
deo 7 huic ecce. Que de dono cui-
dam regine Alie'nore optinuerat
eim a co'scolares i sua inuentute ex'titio
et sodales. fuerat aut gema Antea ipi
regine A. In una q pte Anuli isculp-
tus R. In alia: A. R: pro Ric. A: p aial.
Pondat aut de'ce den. de Anulo epi Iohis.

Hunc Anulu dedit deo cum magno
et huic ecce dns Iohis Saphir o.
epe qdam Ardferten'sis. In cui'
castone otinet' saphir' eiam orien-
tal' pulchru mueq; magnitud'is;
quatuor tenacul' que uulgarit' pcom'
dicunt co'iuseptus. Qui dico saphir' p'
eq'uor Angulos i una i'surgit i medio
su'mitate. Deputatur p'cipuis festiuitatibq; Inscribiturq; hoc nome iohis.
Ponderat autem. xviii. den.

Hunc lapide i' p'ciosu de peridco
qui uulgarit' di peridos. Qui et
subuiridis coloris est. Et in cui' medio saphir' mire pulchritud's collocat'
ur. 7 h' nome Iohs intelal't i'sculp-
itur: dedit dns Iohs epe qda Ardstni'
deo 7 huic ecce. pforatur au'. et virtute h' spasmu potuit refrenandi. Et utiq;
forma fere clupeale. Et pondat vi. den.

Hunc lapide i' p'ciosu de Saphiro et
videl; saphiru orientale de'm epi.
dedit deo 7 huic ecce pie recordaci-
onis memorie dns Iohs epe qda
Ardstni'. In cui' castone oblongo
et fere tangulari dns saphir' co'tinet'.
In longu 7 i eius su'mitate pforatur.
Casto au' hac notula signatur.
Pondat au' ser den. Hec 7 alia multa
bona co'tulit dns epe huic ecce. q' aliubi
diligens p'scrutator inuenire p'urit anno.

Hunc anulu de magno anulo
nobilissimu rotundu 7 gema
maria 7 ope p'ciosu. In cui'
medio saphir' remissi coloris ine iii. aureos flosc'ulos
collocat'. 7 i eculeu' ei octo gem-
ge. qtuor. s. p'le. 7 qtuor g'nate: dedit
dns henr' epe Winton fr' dni Angl' regi'
deo 7 huic ecce. ad memoria sui i eade
p'petuanda. Ipsius q' nome sc'ibit' ecu-
lo Anuli. Assignat' au' ornatui abb'is
p'cipuis festiuitatibq; Pod'at' q' xxviii. d.

Hunc lapide p'c-
iosu qvidel;
co'stat ex sar-
donice cal-
cedonio et
onice. p'
hoc qd in
ti'sec' la-
tet veru'
ipe totu'
uulgarit'
kaadman
appellat' de-
dit deo 7 ecce

16, 17 *On the Laws and Customs of England*. One of the most notable features of medieval England was its sophisticated legal system. An indispensable guide to this system is a work entitled *On the Laws and Customs of England*, which was attributed to Henry Bracton (died 1268), a royal judge, but probably incorporates the work of several other people. Shown at the top is one of the earliest manuscripts of this treatise. The miniature of a king with, on one side, some soldiers and, on the other, a group of lawyers, echoes the opening words of 'Bracton': 'Two things are necessary for a king who rules rightly, arms and laws'. By a remarkable chance, a notebook apparently used in the compilation of this treatise has survived and is illustrated below.

[Add. MS 11353, f.9]
[Add. MS 12269, f.108]

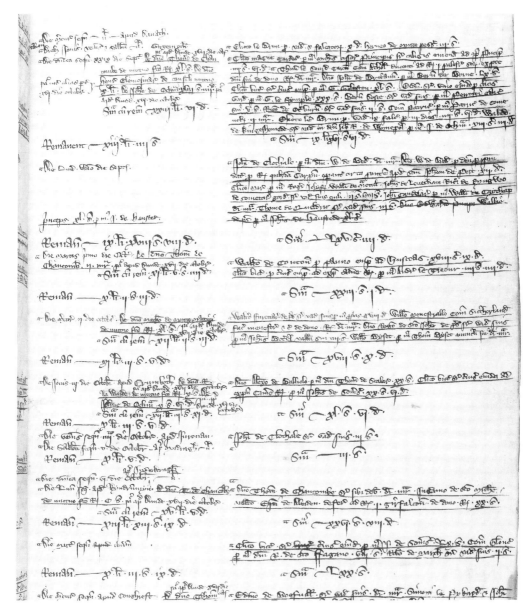

18 Edward I in Scotland.

These accounts record daily receipts and payments by the wardrobe, the department of the royal household which was responsible for organising military supplies and acted as a war treasury, during the campaign of Edward I (reigned 1272–1307) in Scotland in 1303. The entries illustrated here cover the period 25 September to 11 October when Edward left Lochindorb in Morayshire, where he had received the submission of the Scottish lords, and, after moving along the coast towards Elgin, headed south along the road to Dundee. The left-hand column gives details of receipts, together with a note of the date and place and the balance remaining at the end of each day. Items of expenditure are listed on the right, with a daily total.

[Add. MS 35292, f.11]

Ous anez bien
or recorder que
quant le Duc
de bretaigne sen
alla dangleterre que le roy
richart et ses oncles eurent
en conuenant quilz le con
forteroient de gens darmes
et sarchiers et lui tindrent
conuenant Combien quil
ne lui en chey pas bien car
ilz lur cmoterent messire
Jehan sarondel a tout deux
cens hommes darmes et
au tant darchiers lesquelz
eurent vne si Dure aduen
ture sur mer quilz furent
perilz et se sauuerent a
grant malaise Messire

hue de mautelee et messire
thomas trinet Et penent
bien pris iiij iiijxx hommes
darmes et sarchiers autat
Et fut par celle Dure fortite
celle armee rompue dont
le Duc de bretaigne sesmer
ueilloit moult grandemet
Et aussi faisoient ceulx de
son conseil de ce que ilz ne
ouoient nulles nouuelles
sangleterre Et ne pouoit
penser ne pmaginer a quop
il tenoit et eust voulchiers
veu quil eust este conforte
car il estoit grandement
et asprement guerroie de
messire oluier de clichin et
de Messire guy de laual de

19 Froissart's *Chronicles*.

The *Chronicles* of Jean Froissart are renowned for their vivid evocation of the age of chivalry. They cover the years 1325 to 1400 and deal mainly with the events of the Hundred Years War. Froissart assiduously sought out and interviewed eye-witnesses of the incidents he describes and his *Chronicles* are full of colourful circumstantial detail. This manuscript was produced in the late 15th century for Edward IV's chamberlain, William, Lord Hastings. The miniature shows an English force led by Edward III's son, Thomas, Earl of Buckingham, landing in France in 1380.

[Royal MS 18.E.I, f.103v]

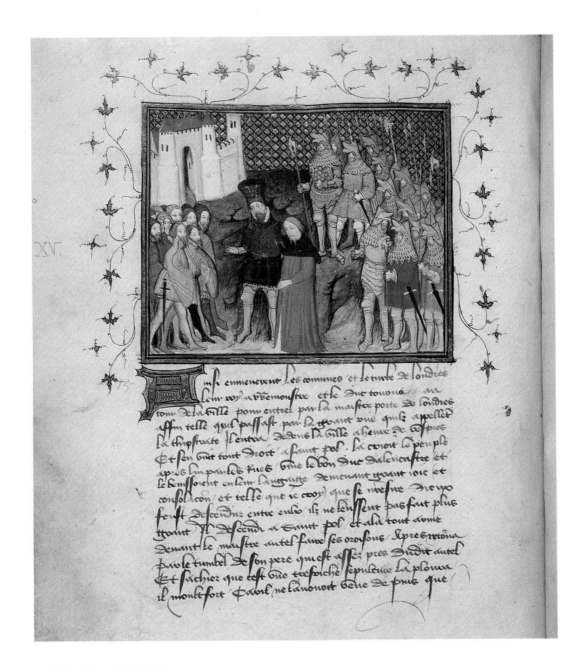

20 Richard II and Bolingbroke.

Jean Creton was a French esquire who went to England in 1399 'for amusement and to see the country' and became caught up in the events leading to the overthrow of King Richard II by Henry Bolingbroke. On his return home, he wrote an account of what he had seen in order to shame Richard's enemies. The miniature on this page from a late 15th-century French manuscript of Creton's work depicts Richard II (with a forked beard and dressed in a red cloak) arriving outside London after his capture by Bolingbroke (the figure in black).

[Harley MS 1319, f.53v]

Ces sunt les nouns des ordenours.

Lerceuesqe de Caunterbiri.
Leuesqe de Loundres.
Leuesqe de salesbiri.
Leuesqe de Cicestre.
Leuesqe de Norbiz.
Leuesqe de Landa.
Leuesqe de sent dauiz.

Le counte de Gloucestr̄.
Le counte de Lancastre.
Le counte de Hereford.
Le counte de Pembrok.
Le counte de Warrewyk.
Le counte de Richemond.
Le counte de Arondel.

Hughe de veer.
Hughe de Courtenay.
William Martin.
Robert le fiuz Roger.
William Mareschal.
Robert de Clifford.

Euesqes.

Countes.

Barons.

Breue missum maiori ⁊ vicecomitibz
London de ordinacioñbz pclamandis.

Edwardus dei gra Rex Angl̄, Dñs
Hibn̄ ⁊ Dux Aquit̄. maiori ⁊ vic
London salutm̄. Mittimus vobis sub
sigillo nostro quasdam ordinaciones per
venerabilem patrem Robtum Cantuar
archiepm ⁊ quosdam epos Ac comites ⁊
Barones de regno nr̄o AD ordinandū
destatu hospicij nr̄i ⁊ regni nr̄i prediti
virtute cuiusdam cōmissionis nr̄e electos
factas ⁊ nobis ostensas. Sapientes ⁊ firmit̄
iniungentes qd ordinaciones illas in ciuitate
predicta publicari ⁊ eas ibidem in omnibz ⁊
singulis suis articulis iuxta tenorem earr
faciatis inuiolabiliter obseruari. Et cū pub
licacionem huiusmodi feceritis, tunc ordina
ciones illas in Aliquo monasterio vel aliquo

loco securo in ciuitate predicta, vbi melius
expedire videritis sub sigillis vr̄is ⁊ sigill
quatuor de probioribz hominibz ciuitatis
illius deponatis ibidem ꝑpetuo conseruand
T̄me ipo apud London quinto die Octobr̄
Anno regni nr̄i quinto.

Jci comencent les ordenaunces faites
par les ordenours auauntditz.

Edward par la grace de dieu
Roi dengleterre seign̄r Dirlan
de ⁊ Dux daquit̄. A touz ceus
as queus cestes lettres ven
dront saluz. Sachez qe come le xvj iour
de marz Lan de nostre regne tierz al hon
de dieu ⁊ pur le bien de nous ⁊ de nostre
Roialme eussoms grantee de nr̄e fraunche
volunte par nos lettres ouertes As prelaz
countes ⁊ Barons de nostre dist Roialme
qil puissent esliue certeynes ꝑsones des
prelaz countes ⁊ Barons de nostre dist
Roialme qil puissent esliue certeynes per
sones des prelaz countes ⁊ Barons de
nostre dist Roialme les queus lour sem
blerent suffisantz de apeler a eux. Et eus
soms auint grantee par mefmes les let
tres a ceux qe fuissent estre esliuz qeus
qil fuissent par les ditz prelaz, countes
⁊ Barons plein poair de ordener lestat
de nostre hostel ⁊ de nostre Roialme de
suister en tiel manere qe lour ordenaunces
fuissent faites Al honour de dieu ⁊ a lon
⁊ au profit de seinte eglise ⁊ a lonour
de nous ⁊ a nostre profit ⁊ au profit de
nostre poeple solom droit ⁊ resoun el ser
ment qe nous feismes a nostre corone
ment seoun plus pleynement est contenu
en nos dites lettres. et honurable piere
en dieu Robert par la grace de dieu Er
cheuesqe de Caunterbiri ꝑrimat de tote

Capitul̄
272

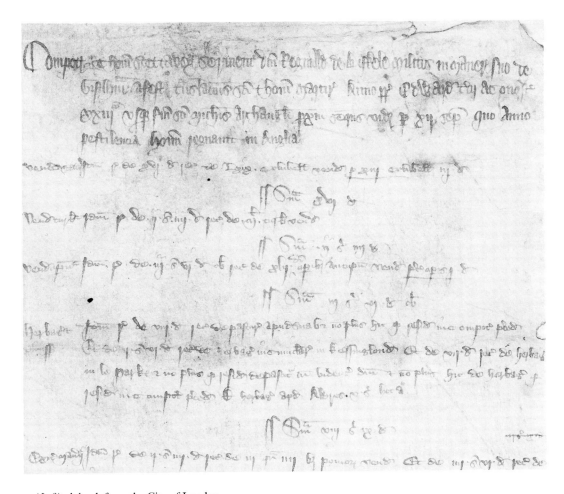

21 (*Left*): A book from the City of London.

Amongst the many medieval town records in the British Library is part of a collection of statutes and other ordinances relating to London bequeathed to the city in 1328 by Andrew Horn, a city chamberlain. This manuscript was broken up at the end of the 16th century. Some folios are now in the custody of the Corporation of London, others at Oxford and the remainder in the British Library. The page illustrated here contains a transcript of the ordinances made in 1311 by a committee of nobles, which Edward II was forced to appoint, with wide-ranging powers to reform the government of the realm.

[Cotton MS Claudius D.II, f.272]

22 (*Above*): A manorial record.

The manor was the basic unit of estate administration in medieval England and the records produced by manorial officials are the main source for English local history in the middle ages. The British Library is one of the chief repositories of such material. These are the accounts of Thomas Scettavey, an official of Sir Reginald de Biskele, lord of the manor of Gisleham in Suffolk, for 7 July to 29 September 1349. This was the time when the Black Death first arrived in England and the heading of the accounts notes that this was 'the year in which the human pestilence reigned in England'.

[Add. Roll 26058]

mas tuitilor z mungdalor.

Magifter Johannes Ap
pelbp tecanus ssi pauli. de
dit huic eccfie unam capa
cui? campus eft unidis. in
quo dinerse beftie auree infernut. pannus ue
ro acta uulganiter appellatur.

Dña Eluzabet te la souche
dedit huic eccfie unñ uefti
mentū. saluct casulam. tu
nicam.z dalmaticam. cū fto
lis z manipulis z trib; albis. quod ueftimen
tum eft te panno albo. quem baltekynū te da
masco nocamus. dorsum uero z pecorale op
time serico texunt z auro. Et tedit quodtam fron
tale p altari pulcrū ssd hetur
Redburne ex dno dñi.G. albis.

Dñs Ricardus te Ghre
ton sacertos. executor dñi
Roberti te Thozp Militis
quondam Regni Cancellarij

23 The 'Golden Book' of St Albans.
The British Library contains the largest single collection of English monastic records.
This is part of a book compiled in 1380 listing gifts made to St Albans Abbey and giving
portraits of each of the abbey's benefactors. Depicted here are John Appleby, a Dean of
St Paul's, Elizabeth de la Zouche and Richard de Threton, a priest.

[Cotton MS Nero D.VII, f.106]

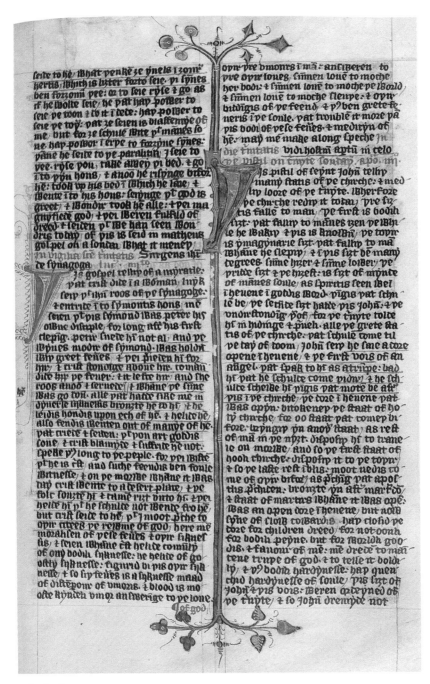

24 Lollard sermons.

The Lollards were followers of the radical theologian John Wycliffe (died 1384), whose criticisms of the church anticipated, in some respects, the views of the reformers of the 16th century. This 15th-century collection of sermons in English gives a vivid insight into their ideas.

[Royal MS 18.B.IX, f.85]

4. Feb,
1444
23 H 6.

25 (*Above*): A Paston letter.
The Paston Letters, the most famous early collection of correspondence in English, are the papers of a well-to-do family from the Norfolk village of Paston. They give a colourful picture of the litigious and often violent nature of life in 15th-century East Anglia. This letter dated 4 February 1445 from the domineering widow Agnes Paston to her son Edmond begins: 'To myn welbelovid sone. I grete yow wel and avyse yow to thynkke onis of the daie of yowre fadris counseyle to lerne the lawe for he seyde manie tymis that ho so ev[er] schuld dwelle at Paston schulde have nede to conne [know how to] defende hym selfe'. [Add. MS 34888, f.13]

26 (*Right*): A letter of Henry V.
This autograph letter of Henry V (reigned 1413–1422), written probably in 1419, orders the unnamed recipient to ensure the safekeeping of the Duke of Orleans and other prisoners taken at the Battle of Agincourt in 1415 and King James I of Scotland, captured in 1406, as Henry had received intelligence of a plot to free them. The last three lines read: 'I wolle that the Duc of Orliance be kept st[i]lle within the castil of Pontfret [Pontefract] with owte goyng to Robertis place or any othre disport, for it is bettre he lak his dispor[t] [t]hen we were disceyved. Of alle the remanant dothe as ye thenketh'. [Cotton MS Vespasian F.III, f.8]

...yow to thynke one of the days of yowr fadrs counseyle
...o on shuld dwelle at Paston shulde have made to
...nd yowr fadr in hewtyn seyd was why the so acordid
...how it wolle be hathe pullid spe the dore and some
...wyl obeye the keye to the nolle drede of the grete class
of yowr fadr copyn londe in tyntche on by yow on
...the yow And now he hathe suffrid the eyne to bow to sette
...he made noter Tosseis dyd galweys why the youtte
...yowr for he was a grete man and a wyse man of the
...the yowre I sende yow the name of the men that hath
...clos in this lettyr I sende yow not this lettyr to make
...leyne that they schulle be made lovys of they keys for
...to have do right werk to that place and that can I speke of
...a good man I sende goddis blessyng I myn Repottyn in hast

...lle ser the parsoo the chapelle at Paston And that
...so ther most be for yowr fadrs wille was as I knowe
...another keye And perowther they pray that thei
...can now selle to havde in this wrytyng And pray to godd
...he and I pray yow to sende me tydyngs how he yow ser

By yowre modyr
Agnes Paston

Anthyrmore I wolle that ye comene wetg my brothyr wetg the chaunceller wetg my cosyn
of northumbrelond and my cosyn of westmorland and that ye set a gode ordinance for my
nortg marches and specialy for the Duc of orliaus and for alle the remanant of my
prysonere of frause and also for the se of scotelond for as I am resly enformyd by
a man of ryght notable gere in this lond that ther gath ben a man of the Duc of
orliaus in scotland and acorded wetg the Duc of albany that this next somer he shal
bryng in the manner of scotland to fette what he may and also that ther schold be
founden weye to the havyng awey spedily of the Duc of orliaus and also of theire
to selle us of the remanant of my forseyd prysonere that god do defende therfore
I wolle that the Duc of orliaus be kept so sure wetg in the casell of pontfret wetg oute
goyng to robert place or to any other disport for it is better he lak his disport
then we were dysseyed of alle the remanant dothe as ye thynketg

27 The hanging of an abbot.

This is a survey by Henry VIII's commissioners of the lands of Colchester
Abbey, compiled in 1540 shortly after the dissolution of the abbey. The Abbot
of Colchester, Thomas Beche, was accused of denying that Henry was the
supreme head of the English church and, despite retractions made by him, was
hanged. The heading of this survey incorporates a copy of a Dutch engraving of
the *Triumph of Mordecai*, which was apparently intended to symbolise the judge
leaving the town after the abbot's trial. In the background can be seen a figure
on a gallows.

[Egerton MS 2164]

The 16th and 17th centuries

Nowadays government documents are looked after very carefully and access to them is restricted. Each government department maintains a register of files and keeps a record of the whereabouts of each file. Detailed regulations govern the selection of material for permanent preservation in the Public Record Office and there are elaborate procedures for the destruction of unwanted papers. It is illegal to disclose the contents of official papers to unauthorised persons. Of course, this does not mean that every important government document is preserved for future researchers. The civil servants responsible for 'weeding' ephemeral papers from files may make injudicious decisions. Occasionally documents embarassing to the government or a particular official may even be illicitly destroyed. Nevertheless, a minister or civil servant who lent official papers to his friends, gave them to autograph collectors or kept them amongst his private papers after he left office would face severe penalties.

This was not the case in the 16th and 17th centuries. Royal ministers rarely made a distinction between public and private papers, often retaining government documents after they had left office and ignoring orders for their return. In many important government offices, such as that of the principal secretaries of state, little attempt was made at systematic record-keeping and documents were left in jumbled heaps in large chests. Officials took papers home and failed to return them. They sometimes also lent documents to interested friends and acquaintances. There was no central record-keeping agency. Each department had its own record keepers, many of whom took little interest in the material in their custody.

Consequently, official papers of this period have been widely dispersed. For example, although many of the papers of William Cecil, Lord Burghley, Elizabeth I's principal minister for most of her reign, and his son, Robert, 1st Earl of Salisbury, secretary of state from 1596 until his death in 1612 and also lord treasurer for the last four years of his life, were returned to the state paper office in Whitehall after Robert's death and are now in the Public Record Office, approximately 30,000 documents were left at Robert's house at Hatfield in Hertfordshire, where they are still preserved. Another group of about 15,000 documents relating to William Cecil's period of office were retained by his secretary, Sir Michael Hickes. After various migrations, these papers were acquired in the 18th century by William Petty, 1st Marquess of Lansdowne and 2nd Earl of Shelburne, were purchased with his collection of manuscripts by the British Museum in 1807 and are now in the British Library (**inside front cover**).

The opportunities created for collectors by such a situation are evident from the library of Sir Robert Cotton, which contains many state papers including much of the diplomatic correspondence of Henry VIII's reign and an important group of documents relating to Henry's ecclesiastical reforms (**30, 32**). Cotton acquired many of these papers as a result of his own political activities. He acted, for example, as advisor and unofficial secretary to the lord privy seal, Henry Howard, 1st Earl of Northampton, and was given access to official documents in connection with this work, which he retained. He also assisted in government inquiries into such subjects as naval administration and royal revenues and this gave him further opportunities to borrow official papers which he added to his collections. Some officials gave documents in their custody to Cotton because they felt that his library was the safest place for such papers. In 1618, James I even gave Cotton permission to remove from the state papers royal and other autographs attached to documents 'otherwise unimportant'. Cotton was not above pilfering documents and some of the official papers in his collection were probably taken illicitly by him or his agents.

Many of the 16th- and 17th-century documents in the Library therefore form part of the national archive. The difficulties at this time in distinguishing between public and private papers and ensuring that official material remained in the government's custody were exacerbated by the emergence of letters and other informal memoranda as the major form of historical document. It can be difficult to decide how far a letter written by a minister should be regarded as a government document, whereas the official character of, say, the plea roll of a court is more readily apparent. Because of the large number of letters which survive from this period, it is easier to obtain a direct insight into the motives and personalities of those involved in the great events of the time than in the middle ages. This is further assisted by the appearance of other more personal forms of historical document such as diaries (35).

This does not mean, however, that the medieval forms of document disappeared. Chronicles, for example, continued to be produced and were a very popular form of literature, but are much less important as historical sources than medieval chronicles. Many of the chief administrative records continued to be compiled in exactly the same way as in the middle ages. During the Tudor period, however, some important administrative innovations were made, giving rise to new types of record, such as parish registers (33, 34).

The introduction of printing did not at first have any substantial impact on the form of historical documents. It simply provided a means of making documents such as statutes more widely available (31). During the 16th century, however, an increasing number of printed pamphlets on a wide range of subjects were produced. Some commented on current religious and political controversies, while others put forward proposals for economic and social reforms. A large number contained moralising reports of such newsworthy events as natural disasters or supernatural phenomena. Eventually in the early 17th century the first newspapers appeared. The production of these early pamphlets and newspapers could be a hazardous business. The council and secretaries of state kept a careful lookout for subversive publications and the court of the star chamber inflicted vicious punishments on those responsible for such literature. Following the abolition of the star chamber in 1641, however, the production of such printed tracts and newspapers flourished.

The Library's holdings of printed books of this period were chiefly built up, like the manuscripts, by great private collectors. Some of these were contemporaries, such as George Thomason, the London bookseller who assembled a huge collection of books and pamphlets printed during the period of the Civil War and Commonwealth (46). Others lived more recently, such as Thomas Grenville (1755–1846), whose library, bequeathed by him to the British Museum, was unusual in that, unlike most collectors at that time, he concentrated on obtaining the best texts in certain fields rather than collecting old books for their own sake. Nevertheless, many of the 16,000 books he acquired are of the greatest rarity and include, for example, 14 Caxtons. Grenville was particularly interested in 16th-century history and amongst the rare books of this period in his collection is the first edition of James I's *Basilikon Doron* (42). Grenville's library also contained a few manuscripts, now incorporated in the Library's Manuscript Collections, such as a resolution of the English naval commanders pursuing the Spanish Armada (40). The Library continues to add to its collections of printed material of this period. The rare printed proclamation of Philip and Mary illustrated below (36) was, for example, purchased as recently as 1971.

28 Henry VII's accounts. One of the means by which Henry VII (reigned 1485–1509) restored the authority and prestige of the crown after the instability of the 15th century was careful financial management. His business-like methods are apparent from this book which records payments between 1502 and 1505 by the chamber, the office of the royal household which Henry developed into a national treasury. Henry personally checked the accounts and wrote against each total his initials 'H.R.'.
[Add. MS 59899, f.29v]

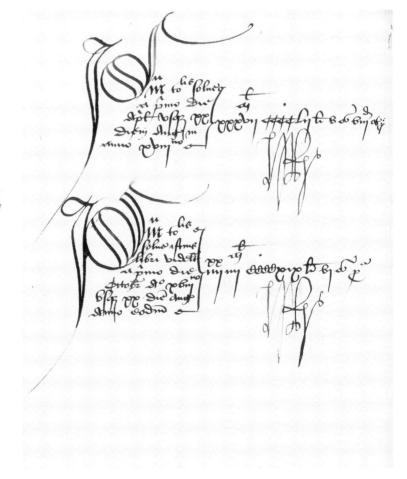

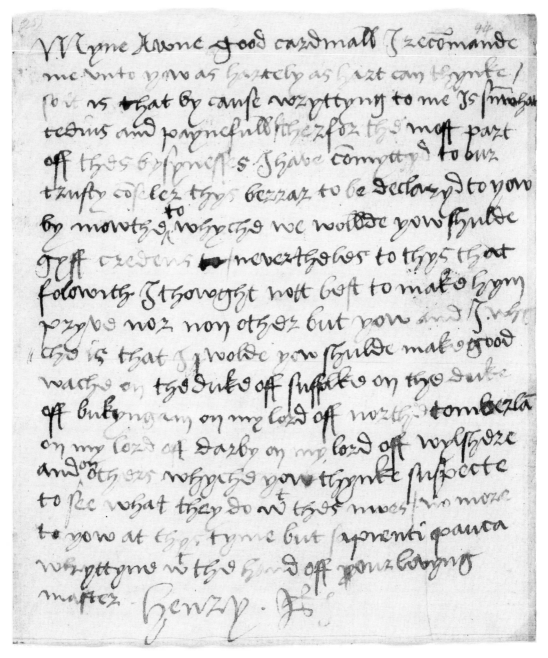

29 A letter of Henry VIII.
Henry VIII (reigned 1509–47) found penmanship arduous and this is a rare example of a letter entirely in his own hand. It dates from late 1520 or early 1521 and was addressed to Cardinal Wolsey, Henry's most powerful minister from 1515 to 1529. From the third line onwards, Henry declares 'that by cause wryttyng to me is su[m]what tedius and paynefull, therfor the most part off thes bysynesses I have co[m]myttyd to our trusty co[un]seler thys berrar to be declaryd to yow by mowthe'. Henry also, however, wanted to advise Wolsey in confidence that he should 'make good wache' on a group of nobles who resented Wolsey's authority.
[Add. MS 19398, f.44]

30, 31 A reformation statute. The *Act in Restraint of Appeals to Rome* of 1533 was the first of the statutes for the reformation of the English church passed under Henry VIII to attack directly the pope's authority in England. Shown above is part of a draft of the act which contains a few amendments by Henry himself. Here, he has inserted the words 'off and frome the sayd imperiall crowne and non other wyse' in order to emphasise that the power of both secular and church courts derived from the king. Below is the opening of the final version of the act from the collection of statutes passed by parliament in 1533 published by the king's printer at the end of the parliamentary session.
[Cotton MS Cleopatra E.VI, f.185]
[Printed Books, 506.d.31.(4)]

¶ An acte that appeles in such cases as hath ben vsed to be pur=
sued to the See of Rome shall not be from hensfozthe
had ne vsed but within this realme. Ca.xii.

Where by dyuers sondzye olde autentyke histozies & cronicles hit is manyfestlye declared and expzessed / that this realme of Englande is an Jmpire, & so hath ben accepted in the wozlde gouerned by one supzeme heed and kynge, hauyng the digni= tie and royall astate of thimperiall crowne of the same: Unto whom a body politike, compacte of all soztes & degrees of people, deuyded in termes and by names of spiritualtie and tempozaltie, ben bounden and owen to beare nexte to god, a naturall and humble obedience, He beynge also institute and furnysshed by the goodnes and suffraunce of almyghtye god, with plenarie, holie, and entire power, pzeeminence, auctozitie, pzero= gatiue, and iurisdiction, to rendze and yelde Justice and fynall determi= nation to all maner of folke resiauntes oz subiectes within this his realme in al causes, matters , debates, and contentions, happenynge to occurre, insurge, oz begyn within the limittes therof, without restreynt oz pzouoca= tion to any fozein pzincis oz potentates of the wozld: The body spirituall wherof hauynge power whan any cause of the lawe diuine happened to come in question, oz of spirituall lernynge, than hit was declared, inter= pzete, and shewed by that parte of the sayde body polytike, called the spiritualtie / nowe beinge vsuallye called the englysshe churche / whiche alwayes hath bene reputed and also founde of that sozte, that boothe foz knowlege, integrite, and sufficiencie of noumbze, hit hathe bene alwayes thought, and is also at this houre, sufficient and mete of it selfe, withoute the intermedlynge of any exteriozpersone oz persones, to declare and de= termine all suche doutes, and to admynister all suche offices and ducties as to theyz rounes spiritualle dothe apperteyne. Foz the due administra= tion wherof, and to kepe them from cozruption and sinistre affection, the
kynges

Aft the Judgement ageynst the Abbott
of and other

And a Comyssyon of Oyer determyner
in to barkshyr ffor his Judgement and
tryall

And Letteys patets to be sent to the
Corem for the ffyrster examynarye
of the abbott of glaster

And lres to be sent wt the copye of
the Judgement ageynst to Jhon
Sayntlowe more aftr the rape and
burgalarye don in Somsetshyre wt the
lorde presydent Russell / wt a Commaundement to procede to Justyce

And the abbott Redyng to be sent
down to be tryed & executyd at
Redyng wt his complyces

It the Abbott of glaster to tryed
at glaster / and also executyd ther wt
his complyces

32 (*Left*): Thomas Cromwell's 'Remembrances'.

Thomas Cromwell (died 1540), Henry VIII's chief minister during the 1530s, was responsible for the implementation of the chief ecclesiastical reforms of Henry's reign and also made some important administrative innovations. This is one of a series of *aide-memoires* or 'remembrances' which Cromwell made to remind him of outstanding business. It is concerned with arrangements for the trials of the recalcitrant Abbots of Reading and Glastonbury in 1539. The last two paragraphs read: 'It[c]m thc abbott Rcdyng to be sent down to be tryed & executyd at Reding w[t] [with] his complycys. It[e]m the Abbott of glaston[bury] to be tryed at glaston[bury], and also executyd ther w[t] his complycys'.

[Cotton MS Titus B.I, f.441]

33, 34 (*Right*): An early parish register.

In 1538, Cromwell ordered that churches should enter in a book details of every baptism, marriage and burial, thus initiating one of the most important series of local records, parish registers. Hardly any original registers of this period survive; most early parish registers are, like this example, late 16th-century transcripts made in response to an order that existing registers, which were mostly on paper, should be copied into more durable parchment books. Shown here are the title page and first entries for burials from the register of St Peter's church in Dunwich, the Suffolk town which has been swallowed up by the sea. The register was rescued from the church shortly before it finally fell into the sea in 1697; its pages have been stained by water.

[Add. MS 34561, ff.1,58]

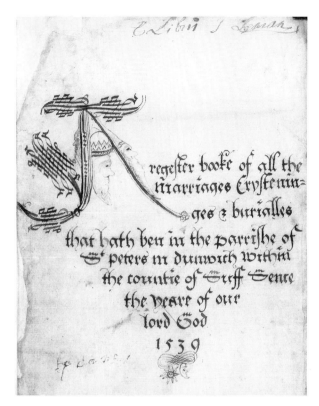

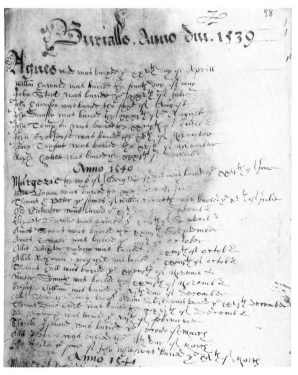

The same day the french King shewed the L
admirall lettres that came from Parma,
how the french men had gotten iij castels
of th'imperials, and in the taking of thes
one the Prince of Macedony was slain on
the walles and was buried w mompe at Parma.
22 The great seale of England deliuered to the bishop of Ely
to be keaper therof during his the L Riches siknes.
23 The bende of ioo men of armis wich my L of
Somerset lare had, appointed to the duke of suthfolke.
23 Removing to Grenwich.
24 I began to kepe haule this Christmas and continewed till twelftyde.
26 S antony Settengers for matters laid against
him, by the bishop of Dublin, was to banyshed, my
court till he had made aunswere, and hade
the articles deliuered him.
28 The L admiral came to Grenwich.
30 Commission was made out, to the bishop
of Ely, to the Lord preuisale S Jhon Gatis,
S wiliam Perre, sir robrt Bowes, and S
walter mildmay for calling in my dettis.

January w the chaundelours
1 Orders was taken w the chaundelours
of London for selling thes talow candels
Wich before some denied to doe, and some
were punished w imprisonement.
3 The chaleng that was made in the last
month was fulfilled. The chalengeurs ware
thirle of warwik.

Defendaunres		
S hary Sidney	The Lord William	The L Fizwarren S Norice
S hary Nouel	The Lord Fizwaren	S G Howard Mr Dygby
S hary Gates	The Lord Ambres	S wil stafford Mr Peartop
	The Lord Robart	S Jhon Perral Mr Courthey

Thies is in all ranne sx courses spece at till against the chalen-
gers, and in thiend accomplished ther courses right well
and so departed againe.

By the kyng and the Quene.

Here as by the Statute made in the seconde yeare of kynge Henry the fourth, concernyng the repzessing of heresies, ther is ozdeyned and pzouided a great punishment, not onely foz the aucthozs, makers, and wzyters of bokes, conteynynge wycked doctryne, and erronious and hereticall opinions, contrary to the catholyque fayth, and determination of the holy churche, and lykewise foz theyz fautours and suppozters, but also foz suche as shall haue oz kepe any such bokes, oz wzytinges, and not make deliuerie of them to the Ozdinarie of the dioces oz his ministers within a certayne tyme limited in the sayde Statute, as by the sayd Statute moze at lardge it doth appeare. Which act oz statute being by auctozitie of parliament of late reuiued, was also openly pzoclamed, to thintent the subiectes of the Realme vpon such pzoclamation should the rather eschue the daunger and penaltye of the sayd Statute, and as yet neuerthelesse, in most partes of the realme, the same is neglected, and lytle regarded.

The kyng and quene, our souerapgne Lozd and Lady therfoze, most entierly, and earnestly tendering the pzeseruation, and saulfty, aswel of the soules, as of the bodyes, landes, & substaunce of al theyz good and louyng subiectes, and others, and mindyng to roote out, and extinguysh al false doctrine and heresies, and other occasions of scismes, diuisions, and sectes that come by the same heresyes and false doctryne, straytly charge, and commaunde, that no person oz persons, of what estate, degree, oz condicion soeuer he oz they be, from hencefozth pzesume to bzynge oz conuepe, oz cause to be bzought oz conueyed into this realme, any boo-

35 (*Left*): Edward VI's diary.
This is a page from the diary of Edward VI, who succeeded to the English throne in 1547 at the age of nine and died six years later. These entries cover the end of December 1551 and beginning of January 1552, when Edward's uncle, Edward Seymour, Duke of Somerset, who had ruled the country for Edward during the first three years of his reign, was in the Tower awaiting execution. Edward does not express any concern about his uncle's fate. The entries for 23 and 24 December, for example, concentrate on preparations for Christmas: '23. Removing to Grenwich. 24. I began to kepe haule this Christmas and continewed till twelftide'.
[Cotton MS. Nero C.X, f.51]

36 (*Above*): A proclamation of Philip and Mary.
On 13 June 1555, Queen Mary I (reigned 1553–8) and her husband, King Philip of Spain, who sought to restore the pope's authority in England, issued this proclamation, which denounces a long list of books as heretical, including the writings of Martin Luther, John Calvin, William Tyndale (the translator of the bible), and the former Archbishop of Canterbury, Thomas Cranmer, who was burnt at the stake in 1556. It also proscribes the Book of Common Prayer issued in Edward VI's reign and orders that all these books be burnt. Only two other copies of the official printed bill advertising this proclamation are known.
[Printed Books, B.g.3.]

1563
Eliz 94:a
See fol:
A Lettre in Queen Elizabeth hand to the Commons in Parliament
about ther petition concerning mariage and Libertie
92

I loue so well counterfaitting and hate so muche dissemulation
that I may not suffer you depart without that
my admonitions may shewe your harmes and cause
shun vnsene perill. Two thinges haue blinded the eyes
of the takers one in this present cession, so farfurth
as vnder pretince of bating the haue done some
good. And these be Succession and liberties. As
to the first, the princes opinion and good wyll ought
in good ordar haue bine felt in other sort than
in so publik a place and to be vttered it had
bine conuenient that so waighty a cause, had had
his original, from a princes cogiderations not
lippe labored orations out of suche subiectes
mouthes wiche what the be time may teache you
knowe and ther demerites wil make them
acknowledge how the haue done ther lewde indevour
to make sall my realme suppose that ther care
was muche whom myn was none at all. ther
handeling of this doth wel shewe the being ignorant
how fit my grant shuld be to suche a demande
maime in one thinge ar of be excusid
for I think this be the first time that
so Waighty a cause passed from so
simple mouthes to liberties Who is so simple that
doutes whither A prince that hed of all the
body may not comaund the fete not to
strean Whan the wold slip God forbid that
or that your lawfull liberties shuld any wais be
yourr libertie but my meaninge
my comaundment
no you were gone beause you haue not
with a gentle prince as your maiesties scruple
bechaunce haue brede your caube blame
Am albeit the douting of suche be reprochable in all
yet I wold not my simplicitie suche
as I can not make distinccions amonge as of bene

37 A speech by Queen Elizabeth.
This is a draft by Queen Elizabeth I (reigned
1558–1603) of a speech made by her at the dissolution
of parliament in January 1567 in which she berated
parliament for repeatedly trying to persuade her to
marry. The most vitriolic passage begins on the eighth
line: 'the princes opinion and good wyll ought in good
ordar have bine felt in other sort than in so publik a
place be uttered. It had bine convenient that so
waighty a cause had had his originall from a zelous
princes co[n]sideration not fro[m] so lippe labored
orations out of suche [the word 'jangling' is deleted]
subjects mouthes'.
[Cotton Charter IV.38(2)]

38 The execution of Mary, Queen of Scots.
This contemporary sketch of the execution of Mary,
Queen of Scots, at Fotheringay Castle in 1587 is from
the papers of Robert Beale (1541–1601), the clerk to
the privy council, who had carried Mary's death
warrant to Fotheringay and read it out immediately
before her execution. This sketch shows Mary at three
different stages of the proceedings: top left, being led
into the hall; in the centre, being prepared for
execution; and top right, being beheaded.
[Add. MS 48027, f.650]

they be of great strength & caste stones agraunde mightily with theire hinder
feet at them which overthrowes them in theire flyeing with great violence they
hurle themselues into the sea & often tymes take theire young ones on theire
back with them. they feed altogether in the day tyme in the sea. the good that
theire oyle is so subtill & peirceth through any
substaunce it is put on. & is a present help for outward inflamacions
in any member whereof divers of our men had good Experience
by my directions to theire great comfortes

Icon Vituli Marini

Vitulus Marinus
This Rock or Iland broader then originall wist. [. . . . .]
& somuch deeper
at least

The Rock or Iland

39 (*Left*): A journal of Drake's circumnavigation of the world. The most detailed account of Sir Francis Drake's circumnavigation of the world between 1577 and 1580 is that of Francis Fletcher, the chaplain of Drake's ship. Only one reliable copy, unfortunately incomplete, of Fletcher's journal survives and this is in the British Library. It was made by the apothecary John Conyers in 1677. This is part of Fletcher's description of an incident in the Bay of Montevideo in which Drake's men killed a large number of seals on a great rock. Fletcher's picture of a seal or 'Vitulus Marinus' (sea calf) on the 'Rock or Iland' has been painstakingly copied by Conyers.
[Sloane MS 61, f.15]

40 (*Above right*): A council of war. This is the resolution of a council of war of the commanders of the English fleet which opposed the Spanish Armada in 1588, made as the Armada tried to escape northwards after the Battle of Gravelines. The English commanders agree 'to folowe and pursue the Spanishe Fleete untill we have cleared oure owne coaste and broughte the Frithe [the Firth of Forth] weste of us, and then to returne backe againe'.
[Add. MS 33740, f.6]

41 (*Below right*): A list of the Armada. This copy of the official Spanish list of the Armada ships belonged to Queen Elizabeth's chief minister, William Cecil, Lord Burghley. Here, he has inserted the name of the Andalusian flagship, the *Nuestra Señora del Rosario*, and notes that 'this shipp was taken by Sr Fra[n]c[is] Drake'.
[Printed Books, 192.f.17.(1)]

A Y en esta esquadra dezifeys nauios, los catorze galeones, y nauios, y dos pa-taxes, que tienen ocho mil fetecientas y catorze toneladas de porte, y estan embarcados en los dichos nauios, dos mil quatrocientos y cincuenta y ocho fol-dados de Infanteria, mil fetecientas y dezinueue perfonas de mar, que fon por to-das, quatro mil ciento y fetenta y fiete, y trezientas y ochenta y quatro pieças de artilleria, y veyntitres mil y quarenta pelotas para ellas, y fetecientos y diez quintales de poluora, y dozientos y nouenta quintales de plomo, y trezientos y nueue de cuerda.

¶ Armada de naues de Andaluzia, de que es Capitan General Don Pedro de Valdes.

Toneladas.	Nauios.	Géte de guerra.	Géte de mar.	Numero de todos.	Pieças de artilleria.	Pelote ria.	Poluora.	Plomo.	Cuerda.
	Nuestra Señora del Rosario.								
1.150	*La nao Capitana.*								
	De Pedro de Leon. 1 11	304.	118.	422.	46.	2366.	114.	11.	10.
	Dõ. Alõ fo de Zayas 1 13								
	De Alõ fo q Pedraza 80								
	‾‾‾								
	304								

45

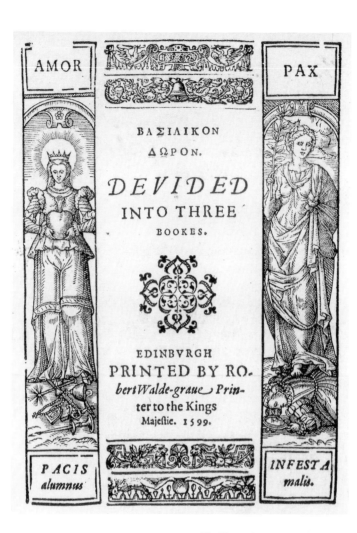

AMOR   PAX

ΒΑΣΙΛΙΚΟΝ
ΔΩΡΟΝ.

DEVIDED
INTO THREE
BOOKES.

EDINBVRGH
PRINTED BY RO-
bert Walde-graue Prin-
ter to the Kings
Majeftie. 1599.

PACIS
alumnus

INFESTA
malis.

42 James I's manual of kingship.

The treatise *Basilikon Doron* (The Gift of a King) was written by James VI of Scotland and I of England (reigned 1603–25) for his eldest son Henry in order to instruct him in the duties of a king. While much of James's advice was sensible and down-to-earth, the book also reflected his view that kings were answerable to God alone. James was at first apprehensive about popular reaction to his ideas and when the first edition of his book was printed in Edinburgh in 1599 only seven copies were produced. This is one of them. The autograph manuscript of *Basilikon Doron* is also in the British Library.

[Printed Books, G.4993]

43 Sir Simonds D'Ewes's parliamentary journal.

According to Thomas Carlyle, these notes are 'the most interesting of all Manuscripts' and enshrine 'what was really memorable and godlike in English history'. They are part of a journal by Sir Simonds D'Ewes (1602–50) of the proceedings of the Long Parliament between 1640 and 1645, the period when the conflict between King Charles I and parliament escalated into civil war. The final paragraph summarises a speech by John Pym, the leading opponent of Charles and his ministers. The third to sixth lines read: '[A] designe to alter the kingdome both in Religion and goverment this is the highest of Treason this blowes upp by peece meales and almost goeth through their ends. This concernes the King as well as wee . . .'.

[Harley MS 162, f.3]

encouragement to preaching printing &c. and advancement but superstitious corrupt in their
doctrines ... and ... in their ... but these Arminians and Popish affected ... which
thrown the Lawes and ... religion and some of both have been the authors of all these miseries
and wee have not ... have the like punishment against them as against Tristilian and
other predecessors &c.

Sr Beniamin Rudiard spake first of Religion and abuses of poore ministers for not reading
the ... booke. They have a minde to quell preaching and to draw the Religion to the
ceremonies this is the forest worke in hand ... let not them say that these are the
sayings of factious people. and à Clara saieth that Puritans were away this Religion
and his would agree. and so they have branded all good Protestants under the name of
Puritans. Some imagining which way wee were tending brought us to ... runne us ... turne
Papists. &c ...

Sr Francis Seymor. Groaning under great burthens. If wee sure all suffer this it were
to betray our duty to the King, and our faith to the Country, & to impoverish the Crowne
The King hath been too provident a King and ... are those that spend. Had they that
have been ... been as provident for the King as for themselves they had not been so
... but the Kings Coffers more full ... of projects but the King had not. and the
... have not been good or else they would not suffer an Army to come to this King
dome. One may see what danger ... in religion Jesuites and Priests openly to walke abroad
and particularly. A priest that was taken ... at first ... slighted will in due time
bee examined. what encouragement is this to our Papists. the law is in execution. for
Papists often to go to Masse. A complaint in our ... ... coughed ... ...
studie more Church dignities then Sermons preached between a Lazy Monke ...
and lazy Priest ... and say to an honest man what what het that troubles us, and ...
they preach. only their owne ... sufferings in goods and persons our liberties taken
from us that is a civill death. none can say hee is a free borne Subiect, things inforced
... off will more then off our lawes, not: by no lawe. Now a question whether a priest
bee a base fellow, but every priest will finde out his owne Master, Law of Allegiance
the ... with a halter about his necke if against ... then to bee hanged
the poore King and Subiect ... poore by ill Counsell ... The great Christians of
the Commonwealth follows Parliaments, and dissolution of them which is the cause of all
mischief. The King hath suffered as much as wee. and I desire that hee may see and heare it
with his owne eyes and eares, and then wee may make Him greater then any; otherwise
looke upon ... all without any end.

Mr. Pymm moved for a reformation &c. finding out authors and punishment of them.
Actuall declaration of offences needed no Statutes and that is a step to reformation. A
desire to alter the Kingdome both in Religion and government this is the highest of Treas
sons this blowes at us by poore meales and almost goods, through their End. This con
cernes the King as well as wee, and that I say with a reverence and care of his Ma. ... See
there are many heads and grievances. 1. The Papists this alter Religion
this is by setting difference betweene the King and his subiects. and ... of Papists
undermine our Religion. 2. The corrupt parts of our Clergie that make ... for their
owne ends and with a union betweene us and Rome. 3. plot Agents for Spaine and other
Kingdomes by correspond to alter Religion and government. 4. Those that are for their owne
preferments and further all bad things are worse then Papists those are willing to runne us
into slavery. Steps of these things that have proceeded in motion first softly now by strides
which are neare their ends if they bee not prevented. designes carried upon fower feete. The
first foot is 1. Ecclesiasticall Courts. 2. Discountenancing of forward men in our Religion
3. Countenancing their owne ... or else no promotion 4. by negotiating Agents from heare
to Rome, and Rome to this place to extirpate our Religion proofe will appeare.
5. frequent preaching for Monarchy ... Lords ... and there ...
2. foote Policy for state and courts of Iustice. 1. The Counsell endeavouring to make
difference between King and people by taxes against Lawes and ... not proceedings
Iudges were ... not granted habeas corpus. in the Kings Bench and wee were ... this
... for our labour.

2.

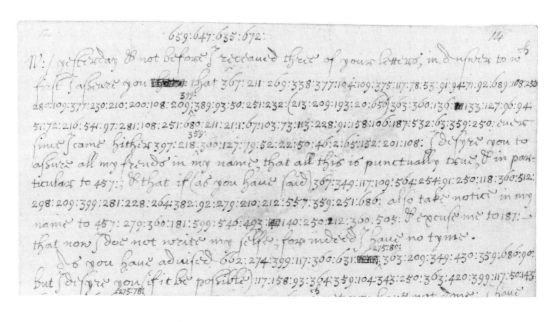

six

1 You ar to accuse those ~~from~~ joyntlie & seuerallie

2 you ar to reserue the power of making addicionall[s]

3 When the Comittie for examinacion is a naming (wch you must presse to be close & under tey of secresie) if eather Essex, Warwick, Holland, Say, ~~████~~ Wharton, or Brooke be named, you must desyre that they may be spared because you ar to examine them as witnesses for me

---

44 (*Above*): The prosecution of the Five Members.

The incident which finally precipitated the outbreak of civil war in 1642 was Charles I's unsuccessful attempt to prosecute Viscount Mandeville and five leading members of the House of Commons for treason. These are Charles's instructions to the attorney-general, Sir Edward Herbert, for the conduct of the proceedings. They show that the prosecution of Mandeville was an afterthought, as his name has been deleted from the list of those Charles intended to call as witnesses and the number of defendants altered from five to six.

[Egerton MS 2546, f.20]

45 (*Below*): A letter in code.

This letter, in a disguised hand and using a numerical cipher, was written by Charles in 1648 while he was a prisoner in Carisbrooke Castle. It was sent to Colonel Silius Titus of the royal household and signed 'J'.

[Egerton MS 1533, f.14]

46 (*Right*): A Thomason Tract.

In 1640, George Thomason (died 1666), a London bookseller, recognising that a major political crisis was developing and wishing to make a record of it, began to collect systematically all the books and pamphlets he could obtain. During the next twenty years, he acquired more than 22,000 items. His collection, now in the British Library, provides a remarkable record of the complex ideological and political cross-currents of the period of the Civil War and Commonwealth. Amongst the many rare items in the Thomason Tracts is this pamphlet giving news of an incident during the siege of royalist forces in Colchester by the parliamentary army in 1648.

[Printed Books, E.456.(11)]

A great and bloudy
FIGHT
AT
Colchester upon Sunday night laſt, and the

ſallying out of Generall *Lucas*, Lieutenant Generall *Haſtings*, and
Colonell *Farr*, with a great Party of Horſe and Foot, upon the Parliaments Forces, cutting off the Perdues, and advancing up to the
Works, with the number that were killed and taken, and their
diſplaying of new ſtratagems by fire. Likewiſe, Gen. *Fairfax* his
Propoſitions to the Soldiery in the Town. And the Princes Reſo-
lution concerning the Army.   Signed,   *Charles P.*

Colcheſter Leaguere.

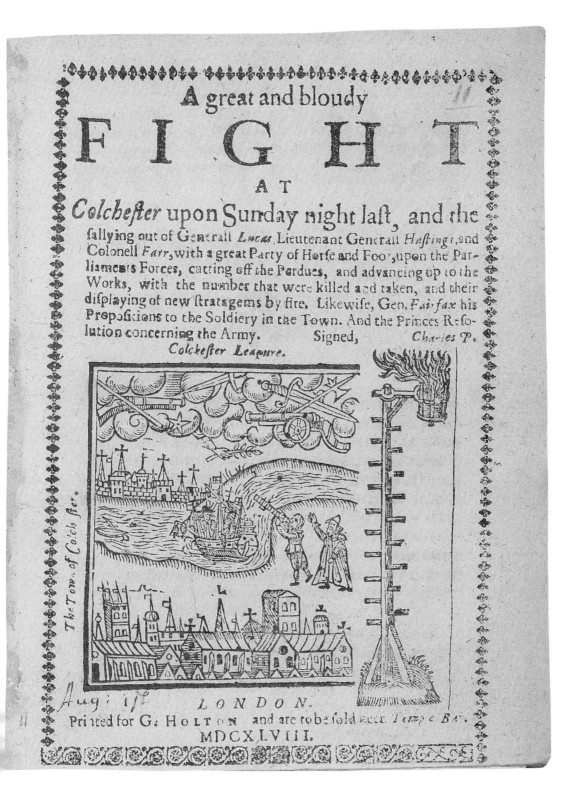

The Town of Colcheſter.

Aug: 1ſt

LONDON.
Printed for G. HOLTON and are to be ſold neer *Temple Bar.*
MDCXLVIII.

The Difeafes and Cafualties this Week.

Abortive	5	Jaundies	5
Aged	43	Impofthume	11
Ague	2	Infants	16
Apoplexie	1	Killed by a fall from the Belfrey at Alhallowes the Great	1
Bleeding	2	Kingfevil	2
Burnt in his Bed by a Candle at St. Giles Cripplegate	1	Lethargy	1
Canker	1	Palfie	1
Childbed	42	Plague	7165
Chrifomes	18	Rickets	17
Confumption	134	Rifing of the Lights	11
Convulfion	64	Scowring	5
Cough	2	Scurvy	2
Dropfie	33	Spleen	1
Feaver	309	Spotted Feaver	101
Flox and Small-pox	5	Stilborn	17
Frighted	3	Stone	2
Gowt	1	Stopping of the ftomach	9
Grief	3	Strangury	1
Griping in the Guts	51	Suddenly	1
		Surfeit	49
		Teeth	121
		Thrufh	5
		Timpany	1
		Tiffick	11
		Vomiting	3
		Winde	3
		Wormes	15

Chriftned	Males — 95 Females — 81 In all — 176	Buried	Males — 4095 Females — 4202 In all — 8297	Plague — 7165

Increafed in the Burials this Week —————— 607

Parifhes clear of the Plague ——— 4   Parifhes Infe&ed ——— 126

The Affize of Bread fet forth by Order of the Lord Mayor and Court of Aldermen, A penny Wheaten Loaf to contain Nine Ounces and a half, and three half-penny White Loaves the like weight.

47 (*Left*): A bill of mortality.
Amongst the key documents for the study of population trends in early
modern England are bills of mortality, which were weekly tables
compiled by the parish clerks of towns such as London showing the
number of deaths registered in each parish and also giving a breakdown
of causes of death. This is the analysis of causes of death from the
London bill of mortality for the week 12–19 September 1665, which
marked the height of the great outbreak of bubonic plague in London
during that year. As can be seen, during this week more than 7,000
people died from plague in the city.
[Printed Books, 1877.e.7]

48 (*Below*): A map of the Fire of London.
This map by John Leeke shows the streets burnt in the Fire of London
in 1666. Only the eastern section of the map is shown here; the area of
destruction extended as far west as Temple Bar.
[Add. MS 5415 E.1]

49 (*Right*): An order of the Fire Court.
Following the Fire of London, disputes arose about such matters as
who was responsible for rebuilding destroyed properties and whether
rent was payable on a property while it lay in ruins. A special court was
set up to settle these questions speedily and the original decrees of this
court are preserved in the British Library. This order concerns a house
and shops on the south side of St Paul's Cathedral which had been
destroyed in the fire.
[Add. MS 5064, f.279]

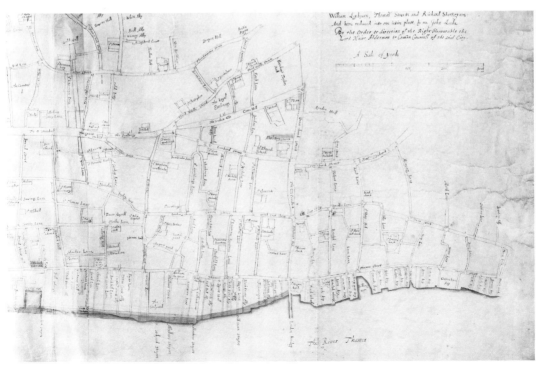

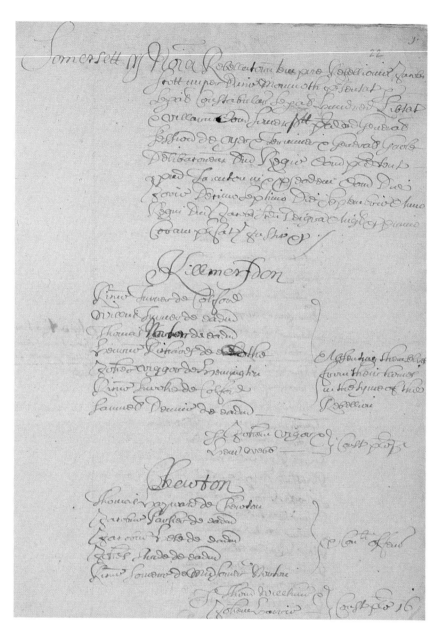

51 The 'Glorious Revolution'. Following William of Orange's invasion of England in 1688 at the invitation of a group of leading Englishmen opposed to James II's pro-catholic policies, a meeting of peers was held at Windsor to decide how James should be dealt with. George Savile, Marquess of Halifax, presided over the meeting and these are his notes of its deliberations. Some Lords wanted to send James to the Tower and, Halifax notes at the foot of this page, 'All spoke against his going to any of his own houses. Would not do anything that might look like treating him as a King'. James was eventually allowed to escape to France.
[Althorp Papers, C.8 (unfoliated)]

50 The 'Monmouth Roll'.

The 'Monmouth Roll' is a return made by local constables in Somerset, Devon and Dorset of those people suspected of joining the rebellion of James, Duke of Monmouth, an illegitimate son of Charles II, against the Roman Catholic James II (reigned 1685–8) in 1685. Shown here is the beginning of the Somerset returns, with the names of suspected rebels in Kilmersdon and Chewton. This document was intended to assist the prosecution of rebels at the 'Bloody Assizes' of Judge James Jeffreys at which more than 300 rebels were sentenced to death and hundreds more condemned to transportation as slaves to the West Indies.

[Add. MS 30077, f.22]

Present.

D. of Grafton.
Ld Macklesfield
Ld Wiltshire
Ld Delamore.
Ld of Stamford.
Ld North.
Ld Churchill.
Ld Mordaunt.
Ld Carbury.
Ld Clarendon
Ld Halifax
Ld Shrewsbury.

Ld Delamore mooved the Tower.
Ld Macklesfield. The same.
Ld Stamford the same
Ld Mordaunt. 2n.
D. of Grafton against it.
Ld Churchill the same.
Ld. Shrewsbury. 2n.

Ld Clar. said it would beare a debate whether
the K. should bee left at liberty.
the whole thing told him, of what had
passed before hee came in.
Hee went and gave particular instructions
about the Avenues at Whitehall for the
house of Comes.
All spoke against his going to any of his
own houses
would not doe any thing that might look like trea
ting him as a King.

52, 53 The Blenheim Dispatch.
One of the most dramatic items in the Library's collections is this note, hastily scribbled in pencil on pages ripped from a notebook, from John Churchill, 1st Duke of Marlborough, (1650–1722) to his wife Sarah, reporting his victory over the forces of the French King Louis XIV and his Bavarian allies at Blenheim in southern Germany in 1704. It begins: 'I have not time to say more, but to beg You will give my duty to the Queen, and let her know Her Army has had a Glorious Victory. Mon^sr Tallard [the French commander] and two other Generals are in my Coach, and I am following the rest'.
[Add. MS 61428, ff.95,95v]

The 18th, 19th and 20th centuries

As has been seen, the Library's manuscript collections for the medieval and early modern periods are dominated by material dispersed from such sources as monastic libraries and the public records. By contrast, the Library's holdings of manuscript historical documents for the modern period consist chiefly of a large number of more or less intact archives. These are mostly collections of personal papers, but they also include some institutional records, such as the archives of the South Sea Company, presented to the Library following the liquidation of the company in 1856 (55). The Library even possesses a few groups of modern official documents apparently not thought suitable for the Public Record Office. Between 1900 and 1905, for example, the foreign secretary gave to the Library two large collections of transcripts of Portuguese and Spanish documents made in connection with disputes over the frontiers of British Guiana.

The earliest major collection of personal papers in the Library is the Paston Letters of the 15th century and the Library also contains some important groups of correspondence from the 16th and 17th centuries. From the late 17th century onwards, however, a greater awareness of the historical interest of personal papers began to develop and a much larger number of such collections have survived. A list of the people whose papers are in the Library reads like a directory of the outstanding personalities of modern British history. They include a number of British prime ministers, ranging from the Duke of Newcastle in the 18th century (59) to Campbell Bannerman in the 20th, as well as many other politicians and civil servants. The papers of nearly a quarter of all the cabinet ministers who held office between 1782 and 1900 are in the British Library. The Library's collections are not limited to the papers of politicians. It also possesses the papers of diplomats such as Lord Harvey of Tasburgh, the British ambassador in France in 1940 (**inside back cover**), of naval and military figures such as Lord Nelson (**63, 64**) or General Gordon (**75, 76**) and of social reformers as diverse in their aims and characters as Francis Place (**67**), Florence Nightingale (**73**) and Marie Stopes (**78–80**).

Some of these collections consist simply of the papers of a single person. Others are family archives whose complex structure reflects the family's history and connections. For example, the papers from Blenheim Palace in Oxfordshire acquired by the Library in 1978 consist chiefly of the correspondence and other papers of John Churchill, 1st Duke of Marlborough, (1650–1722), his wife, Sarah and their son-in-law, Charles Spencer, 3rd Earl of Sunderland, whose descendants by his second wife Anne Churchill inherited the Dukedom of Marlborough (**52, 53**). The collection contains smaller groups of material relating to later Dukes of Marlborough, sometimes including papers of their staff and associates. There are also some papers of Sunderland's father, Robert, 2nd Earl of Sunderland, a secretary of state under Charles II and James II and an advisor to William III, and of George Digby, 2nd Earl of Bristol, the 2nd Lord Sunderland's father-in-law. Elizabeth, the daughter of Thomas, 2nd Baron Trevor of Bromham, married the 3rd Duke of Marlborough, and this connection brought to Blenheim some Trevor family papers including three further sub-archives: some papers of the Boteler family, whose estate at Biddenham in Bedfordshire was acquired by the 4th Lord Trevor; a few papers of the Hampden family, which was related to the Trevors; and correspondence and literary papers of Sir Richard Steele, the essayist, whose daughter Elizabeth was the wife of the 3rd Lord Trevor. The provenance of two other small collections of papers in the Blenheim archive, one relating to Thomas Brudenell, 1st Earl of Cardigan and the other to Sir John Wildman, the 17th-century revolutionary and postmaster-general, is uncertain.

The contents of these collections of modern papers are extremely varied. They consist mostly of personal correspondence, but almost any other type of document can also be found. The Blenheim papers, for example, include, apart from letters of all kinds, a large number of diplomatic documents ranging from instructions for envoys to articles of agreement for treaties, newsletters and printed news-sheets, military journals, lists of parliamentary divisions, drafts of literary works, maps and plans, personal accounts, official letter books, contracts and elevations connected with the building of Blenheim palace, passports and many petitions. There is also a considerable quantity of printed material, ranging from pamphlets by Daniel Defoe and others to a single sheet containing some *Directions for using the warming machine.*

Collections of private papers may also contain substantial numbers of official documents, so that, as in the 16th and 17th centuries, the Library holds an important part of the national archive. For example, the series of books containing summaries of dispatches received and sent out by the foreign office compiled from 1789 for the use of the foreign secretary were regarded as the private property of the foreign secretary and retained by him when he left office. The official letter books of such foreign secretaries as Lord Grenville, Lord Aberdeen and Lord Palmerston are consequently to be found in the British Library rather than the Public Record Office. Similarly, 19th-century cabinet papers are mostly only preserved in collections of private papers such as those in the British Library (**70**).

In 1982, the Library became responsible for the administration of a group of records which are still formally part of the public records, the India Office Records. The Library holds these records by permission of the lord chancellor, who is the custodian of the public records, and, unlike the rest of the Library's collections, they are subject to the provisions of the public record acts. The India Office Records consist of the archives of the East India Company and its successors as the governing bodies of the Indian sub-continent, the Board of Control and the India Office, together with the records of the Burma Office and some files of the Government of India. They contain chiefly the records of the London-based officials of the East India Company and its successors, together with documents sent to London through various official channels for the information of the home administration (**63**). The India Office Records are supplemented by the India Office Library, which originated as the staff reference library of the East India Company and the repository for the various books and

54 A log-book of Captain Cook.

The Library contains a large collection of material relating to the voyages of Captain James Cook (1728–1779). This is the entry for 19 April 1770 in the log-book of the ship in which Cook made his first voyage around the world, the *Endeavour*, recording Cook's first sighting of the previously unknown eastern coast of Australia. The first column gives the hour of the day and the second and third columns the speed of the ship. At about 6 p.m., Cook notes, he 'Saw the land extending from N.E. to West'.

[Add. MS 27885, f.18v]

manuscripts received by the company. It is now one of the leading centres for South Asian research. Its collections include the personal papers of many British people with Indian connections (**74**).

At the core of the Library's collections of modern printed material is another archive of a completely different nature. These are the books deposited in the Library in accordance with the copyright acts, which stipulate that a copy of every work published in the United Kingdom, with some minor exceptions, shall be given to the British Library and certain other institutions. This privilege dates back to the transfer of the old Royal Library to the British Museum in 1757, but little was done to enforce it until the mid-19th century. From this time on, the Library's collections constitute an archive of modern printed material, not only for Britain but for many of its former colonies as well. The material of use to historians acquired by the Library in this way is extremely wide-ranging, but perhaps of special interest are ephemeral publications, such as magazines published by local groups, which often vividly convey the atmosphere of a particular period and can be difficult to obtain elsewhere (**82**). Two special categories of material obtained through legal deposit which are fundamental sources to modern historians are newspapers (**84**) and government publications (**62**). The Library's acquisitions of modern printed material do not, of course, consist entirely of material received through legal deposit. It continues to attempt to fill gaps in its 18th- and 19th-century collections through purchase and seeks to acquire all foreign literature of research value, which includes a great deal of material relating to English history (**85, 86**).

55 The 'South Sea Bubble'.
In 1720 a scheme of the South Sea Company to convert the national debt into shares in the company created a wave of reckless investment, finally causing a disastrous financial crash. These calculations of the size of the national debt are from the minutes of the company's court of directors. They continue for another page and purport to show that the debt which the company intended taking over amounted to more than £30 million.
[Add. MS 25498, f.160]

56 South Sea mania.
This letter of April 1720 from Erasmus Lewis to Robert Harley, 1st Earl of Oxford, comments on the South Sea mania gripping the country at that time. Lewis writes: 'I have heard but one sound these three months in this place, viz. that of South Sea, wch has got the Better of Mens Politicks and Lady's fashions, and has entirely engross'd all conversation'.
[Loan MS 29/205 (unfoliated)]

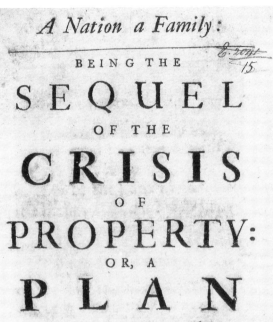

A Nation a Family:

BEING THE

SEQUEL

OF THE

CRISIS

OF

PROPERTY:

OR, A

PLAN

For the IMPROVEMENT of the

South-Sea PROPOSAL.

By Sir *RICHARD STEELE*, Knt. Member of Parliament.

LONDON: Printed for *W. Chetwood*, under *Tom's Coffee-house* in *Covent-Garden*; *J. Roberts*, near the *Oxford-Arms* in *Warwick-lane*; *J. Brotherton*, at the *Black Bull* in *Cornhill*; and *Charles Lillie*, at the Corner of *Beaufort-Buildings* in the *Strand*.   Price **6**d.

58 A caricature from a provincial newspaper. Newspapers are an important historical source for the 18th century. This caricature, from the *Northampton Mercury* of 5 December 1720, illustrates the popular resentment against dealers in stocks caused by the bursting of the 'South Sea Bubble'. The caption suggests that a 'stockjobber' hung from a gibbet would make an admirable sundial.

[Newspaper Library]

57 A pamphlet on the South Sea scheme.
Much political debate in the 18th century was conducted by the publication of pamphlets. Sir Richard Steele (1672–1729), the famous essayist, published two pamphlets in February 1720, *The Crisis of Property* and *A Nation A Family*, in which he argued that the government's creditors were being treated unfairly and ridiculed the proposals of the South Sea Company. This is the title page of *A Nation A Family*, which contains Steele's most detailed criticisms of the South Sea scheme.

[Printed Books, 1093.b.59]

59 The first prime minister.

Sir Robert Walpole (1676–1745), dominated British politics between 1721 and 1742 and is considered to have been Britain's first prime minister. This letter from him to his associate Thomas Pelham-Holles, 1st Duke of Newcastle, was written in the 1720s and begins: 'Yʳ messenger gave me yʳ letter in the feild a hunting, wᶜʰ indeed I did not vouchsafe to open till I came home. That any man could think Politicks should take place wᵗʰ a hare a foot!'. [Add. MS 32686, f.440]

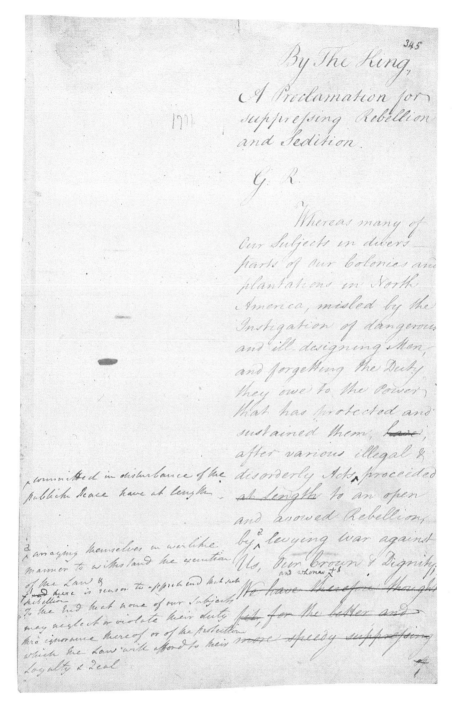

345

By The King,

A Proclamation for suppressing Rebellion and Sedition.

G. R.

Whereas many of Our Subjects in divers parts of our Colonies and plantations in North America, misled by the Instigation of dangerous and ill designing Men, and forgetting the Duty they owe to the Power, that has protected and sustained them, ~~have~~, after various illegal & disorderly Acts, proceeded ~~at length~~ to an open and avowed Rebellion, by levying War against Us, Our Crown & Dignity, and whereas &c

committed in disturbance of the publick Peace have at length.

& arraying themselves in warlike manner to withstand the execution of the Law & ~~and there is reason to apprehend such rebellion~~ To the End that none of our Subjects may neglect or violate their duty thro' ignorance thereof or of the protection which the Law will afford to their loyalty & Zeal

We have ~~therefore thought fit,~~ for the ~~better and more speedy suppression~~

60 A proclamation against the American rebels.
This is the final draft of a proclamation issued by King George III on 23 August 1775 declaring that 'divers parts of our Colonies and plantations in North America' had 'proceeded to an open and avowed Rebellion' and ordering all loyal subjects to resist them. The issue of this proclamation marked the official beginning of the American War of Independence. [Add. MS 34412, f.345]

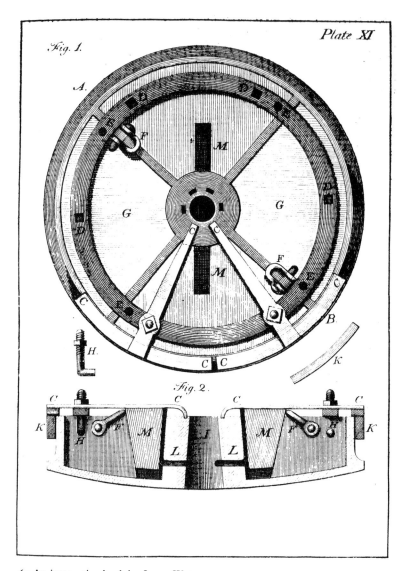

Fig. 1.

Plate XI

Fig. 2.

61 An instruction book by James Watt.
The Library's holdings of 18th and 19th century technical literature provide a record of the inventions and technological developments which facilitated the industrial revolution in Britain. This is a plate from the *Directions for erecting and working the newly-invented steam engines* published by the engineer James Watt (1736–1819) and his partner, Matthew Boulton, in about 1780. The plate contains a plan and cross-section of the engine's piston. The engines manufactured by Boulton and Watt at this time incorporated a separate steam condenser invented by Watt and were much more efficient than earlier steam engines. Watt went on to make many more improvements to his engines, so that they were able to provide the motive power for industrialisation in England.
[Science Reference and Information Service]

62 A report on child labour.
The spread of the factory system and the growth of new industrial centres created many social problems. Illustrated is part of the evidence collected by a royal commission on the employment of children in factories which reported in 1833. The findings of this commission led to an act prohibiting the employment of children under nine and restricting the working hours of older children. Parliamentary papers such as this, of which the British Library possesses a comprehensive collection, are a fundamental source of information about all aspects of modern British history.
[Official Publications and Social Sciences Services]

MANCHESTER.

CHILDREN.

MARY B., aged twelve; ANN O., aged thirteen; MARY F., aged eleven; ANNE J., aged eleven; JANE L., aged eighteen; examined *, but not on oath.

Manchester.

Mary B.

MARY B., aged twelve, class fourteenth: has weak and watery eyes; does not know what it comes from; was so from the first; was a silk winder for four years; at that time worked from six in the morning till seven in the evening; had half an hour for breakfast, an hour for dinner, and half an hour for bagging, which means tea. Is now a back-tenter, and has been for eight or ten months. Her hours are from half past five in the morning to seven in the evening; has half an hour for breakfast, an hour for dinner, but no bagging. Finds back-tenting closes up her health more than silk-winding; thinks this comes from harder work and longer time.

Ann O.

ANN O., aged thirteen, class sixteenth: was twelve months in card-room first; has been a power-loom weaver between two and three years; card-room work hardest; then was stuffed up in her breath; had to fight for her breath every night when she came home. Her hours were from half past five A. M. to seven P. M.; half an hour to dinner, none for bagging (tea). Her wages in card-room were 5s. 1½d. a week; now is a power-loom weaver; works at ———; are about twenty small hands in her room; they work under an overlooker, a man. When girls neglect their work, he threatens to bag 'em.
What do you mean by bagging them?—Why, to send them away. Overlooker has never struck her; has seen him strike other girls with his hand; don't think he hurts 'em so ill; many times blackguards us and curses us; sometimes may strike two or three girls in a week; sometimes never touches us; has the same hours, now that she weaves, as before in the card-room. Weaving agrees with her better than the card-room, but has not good health. A year ago her mother, thinking weaving did her harm from standing on the damp flags, put her back to the card-room; but it stuffed her breath again, and she had the jaundice, and after two or three months mother put her back to weaving again. Has just had an inflammation in the chest; was ill for seven weeks, owing to being damp under foot in the weaving-room, she thinks; has been well a fortnight; wages 8s. and 9s. a week; we are paid according to work; the harder we work, the more we get.

Mary F.

MARY F., going eleven years old, class fourteenth; is a piecer, in ———'s mill; her master is J. F., who is her uncle; gets 3s. 2d. a week wages, and "her twopence besides;" has no father nor mother, her father has been dead ten years, and her mother two months; her uncle gives her wages to her grandmother; her grandmother puts her twopence† by for her, to save it up. Her hours are from half past five A. M. to seven P. M.; half an hour for breakfast, one hour for dinner, no bagging. There are in her room nine pair of mules, nine spinners to the mules, five piecers to each spinner; total, forty-five piecers, or "little hands," in her room. Her uncle never scolds her; has only been at ——— a week; has only worked for her uncle a week; hears other spinners swear very bad at their Spinners swear at their piecers and lick them. piecers; sees 'em lick 'em sometimes, some licks 'em with a strap, some licks 'em with hand; some straps is as long as your arm; some is not that long (here I folded paper to ascertain the width, and so ascertained that it was about an inch and three quarters wide); some is very thick, and some 's thin, a quarter of an inch thick (here I measured on my nail, to ascertain the thickness, and she decided upon about a quarter of an inch as the thickness of the thickest strap). Don't know where they get the straps; sometimes they cut 'em off the drum straps; has never seen one with a handle; there is an overlooker to the room; he very seldom comes in; they won't allow 'em if they knows of it. (The child volunteered this last observation without any question from me.) I asked her how she knew that the overlookers would not allow the spinners to lick the little Not allowed by overlookers. hands: she answered, "Because I've heard 'em say so." Master never comes into her room;

---

* I have suppressed the names of these children, at the suggestion of several operatives who think that it is desirable.

† N. B. The parents or relations always take all the children's wages, and children scarcely ever have them; but at the end of the week the master gives his piecer twopence. This is known by the name of "the piecer's twopence," and it is considered the severest punishment not to give it to them.

(D. 1.)　　　　　　　E　　　　　　　room;

63 The 'Nelson touch'.

On 9 October 1805, twelve days before the Battle of Trafalgar, Horatio,
Viscount Nelson (1758–1805) sent to his second-in-command, Admiral
Collingwood, this draft of his plan of attack, which he called the 'Nelson touch',
for the forthcoming engagement with the French fleet. The essence of Nelson's
plan, which was a masterpiece of naval strategy, is indicated at the bottom of
the right hand page. The fleet was to be drawn up 'in two lines of sixteen ships
each with an advanced squadron' of eight of the fastest sailing ships. The
intention was, as Nelson states on the left hand page, 'to overpower [the enemy
line] from two or three ships ahead of their Commander in Chief supposed to
be in the Centre to the Rear of their Fleet'. This document is exhibited in the
Library's galleries in a frame made of oak from Nelson's ship, the *Victory*.
[Add. MS 37953, f.1]

64 Nelson's last letter.

This was the last letter Nelson wrote. It was addressed to his mistress, Emma, Lady Hamilton, and begun on board the *Victory* on 19 October 1805, two days before the Battle of Trafalgar. Nelson informs Lady Hamilton that the enemy fleet was coming out of port and says that he hopes to live to finish the letter. In a postscript dated the following day, shown here, he describes the enemy ships and concludes 'May God Almighty give us success over these fellows and enable us to get a Peace'. Lady Hamilton has written below 'This letter was found open on *His* Desk & brought to Lady Hamilton by Capⁿ Hardy. Oh miserable wretched Emma. Oh glorious & happy Nelson.'

[Egerton MS 1614, ff.125v–126]

65 Greville's diary.
This entry, for 2 March 1831, from the famous political diary of Charles Greville (1794–1865) describes the introduction in the House of Commons on the previous day of the unsuccessful first bill of Lord Grey's government for parliamentary reform. 'To describe the curiosity the intensity of the expectation & excitement would be impossible,' writes Greville, '& the secret had been so well kept, that not a soul knew what the measure was (though most people guessed pretty well) till they heard [it]'.
[Add. MS 41103, f.89]

66 The passing of the Reform Bill.
Henry Fox, 3rd Lord Holland, (1773–1840) was a member of Grey's cabinet and acted as one of the commissioners to give the royal assent to the reform bill eventually passed in 1832. In this entry from his diary for 7 June 1832, he wrote: 'I sat as one of the Commissioners to pass The Reform bill – we were six in our Robes & on the bench – & I reflected with some satisfaction that five of us were members of the old opposition who uniformly maintained the principles of peace & reform . . .'.
[Add. MS 51869 (unfoliated)]

To the People.

CONFIDENCE in the **KING**, for every act in his reign displays attention to his People's wants.

CONFIDENCE in his Ministers, for they have pledged themselves to stand or fall by the Bill; but above all CONFIDENCE in OURSELVES, for a zealous co-operation will ensure us all we want.

At the last Elections the People of Great Britain came forward with one accord: and the poor man who voted away his franchise, and the rich man who offered up his borough, alike gladly sacrificed self-interest to their Country's cause.

If we continue to pull together, the Country's cause is won.

In every populous District Reformers of all classes have united together, against the Common Foe.

Why is LONDON backward? or, rather, why is not LONDON united into ONE COMPACT UNION, and with all minor differences forgotten, a firm front exhibited, that shall laugh to scorn all the *Lawn Sleeves* and *Ermine*, in Europe.

The Reform Bill is the first step towards Cheap Government, whoever then is for Cheap Government, Blank Pension Lists, and Abolition of Monopolies, let him join the

NATIONAL
Political Union.
Sir F. BURDETT Bart, M.P. Chairman,

THE FIRST PUBLIC MEETING,
WILL BE HELD

On MONDAY next, 31 October 1831,

The Chair will be taken at ONE o'Clock, precisely.

N.B.—Persons will be in attendance to receive the Names of those desirous of becoming Members.
Subscription:—ONE SHILLING PER QUARTER.

POPLETT, Printer, 23, Milton Street.

---

67 The Place Papers.

The attempts of the Tories led by the Duke of Wellington to prevent parliamentary reform caused widespread protest. One of the leaders of the campaign to 'Stop the Duke' was Francis Place (1771–1854), a London tailor. Place's papers, now in the British Library, include a huge collection of newspaper cuttings, posters and other material relating to social and political issues which particularly interested him. This is a handbill of the National Political Union, one of the organisations pressing for reform in which Place was active, issued soon after the defeat of the second reform bill by the '*Lawn Sleeves* and *Ermine*' of the House of Lords.

[Add. MS 27791, f.42]

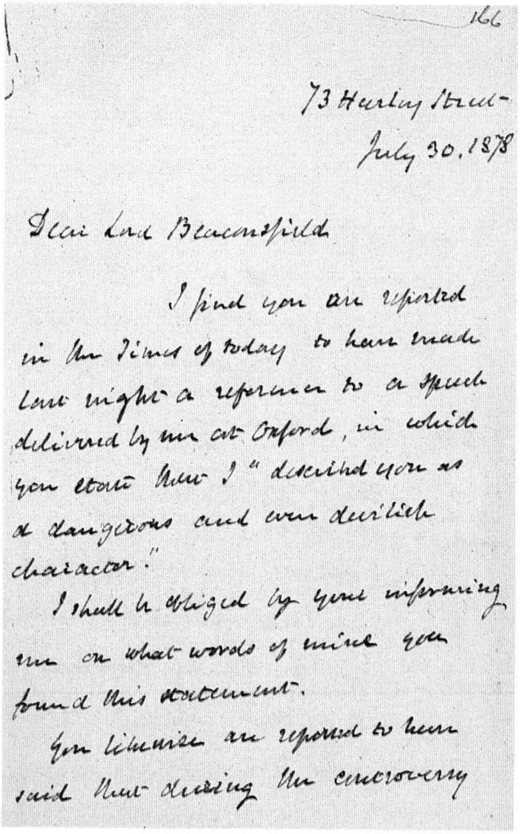

73 Harley Street
July 30. 1878

Dear Lord Beaconsfield

I find you are reported in the *Times* of today to have made last night a reference to a speech delivered by me at Oxford, in which you state that I "described you as a dangerous and even devilish character".

I shall be obliged by your informing me on what words of mine you found this statement.

You likewise are reported to have said that during the controversy

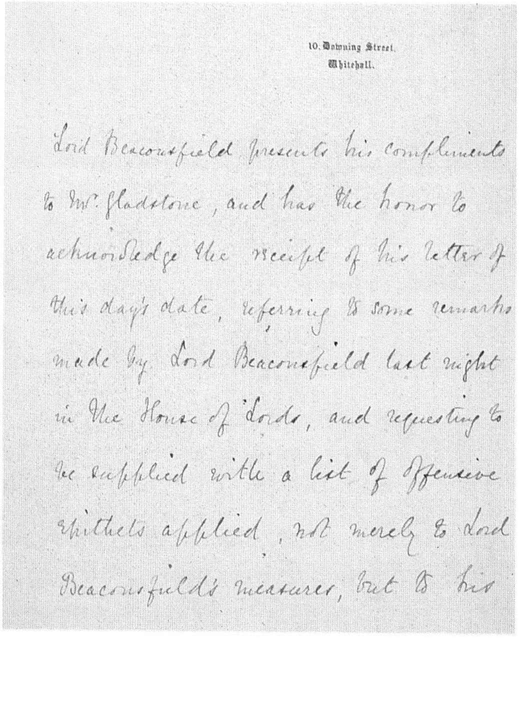

10. Downing Street.
Whitehall.

Lord Beaconsfield presents his compliments to Mr. Gladstone, and has the honor to acknowledge the receipt of his letter of this day's date, referring to some remarks made by Lord Beaconsfield last night in the House of Lords, and requesting to be supplied with a list of offensive epithets applied, not merely to Lord Beaconsfield's measures, but to his

68, 69 The Gladstone Papers.
The British Library possesses the papers of nearly half the prime ministers who held office in the 19th century. Illustrated here are some items from the papers of William Gladstone (1809–98). This exchange of letters between Gladstone and the Conservative leader, Benjamin Disraeli, 1st Earl of Beaconsfield, took place in 1878. Disraeli had claimed that Gladstone had described him as 'a dangerous and even devilish character'. Gladstone asked Disraeli to inform him 'on what words of mine you found this statement'. Disraeli replied that these were innumerable and that, as he was busy, his assistants were undertaking the necessary researches. He did, however, cite instances where Gladstone had accused him of debasing 'the great name of England' and acting duplicitously.
[Add. MS 44457, ff.166,168]

MEMORANDUM BY MR. FORSTER

OF

SUGGESTIONS FOR CONSIDERATION IN FRAMING THE EDUCATION BILL FOR ENGLAND.

In framing an Education Bill, we must first consider why a Bill is demanded.

We are called upon to consider the conditions of our educational vote, and to change our educational system, not because we pay too much money, nor yet because the money is thought to be badly spent, but because the nation does not get what it wants—a complete national system. Notwithstanding the large sum voted for education, there are vast numbers of children utterly untaught, or very badly taught, because there are too few schools, because many schools are bad schools, and because many parents either cannot or will not send their children to school.

Our aim, then, must be,—

(1.) To cover the country with good schools;

(2.) To get the parents to send their children to school.

To hope to fully attain these objects would be utopian, but the public desires and aims at them, and will try and judge our measure according to the progress it makes towards them.

Our first problem, then, is how to obtain complete and efficient school-provision, and in trying to solve it we may surely take it for granted that there are three necessary conditions of any solution.

The Government is called upon to spend public money in aiding the parent to do his duty, and it is also required to remedy the defects in the present system, which being, as it were, a mere partnership with educational volunteers, leaves undone all the work which the volunteers do not care to undertake; but clearly, with this expenditure and this change, there ought to be, consistently with due efforts for attainment of the object,—

1. The least possible encouragement to parents to neglect their duty:

2. The least possible expenditure of the public money:

3. The least possible injury to existing efficient schools.

Our object, then, being to supplement the present voluntary system, that is to fill up its gaps, at least cost of public money, with least loss of voluntary co-operation, and with most aid from the parents, let us consider the four different plans before us:—

(1.) The plan just propounded at Birmingham, which provides that local authorities shall es-

70 (*Left*): A cabinet paper.
Before 1916 there was no cabinet secretariat and the memoranda printed for consideration by the cabinet survive only in the private papers of ministers such as Gladstone. This discussion paper on the drafting of an education bill was produced for Gladstone's cabinet in 1869 by William Forster. The Education Act passed the following year was the first to make provision for universal elementary education.
[Add. MS 44611, f.99]

71 (*Above*): A cabinet minute.
Similarly, before 1916 there were no formal agendas for cabinet meetings and minutes were not kept. The only records of cabinet discussion were the personal letters sent by the prime minister to the sovereign and the private notes of cabinet ministers. These are Gladstone's notes on the cabinet meeting of 10 November 1869 in which Forster's paper on education was discussed (item no. 5).
[Add. MS 44637, f.113]

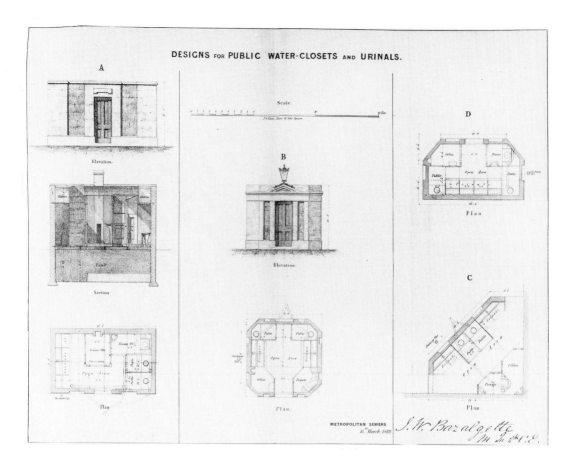

DESIGNS FOR PUBLIC WATER-CLOSETS AND URINALS.

72 (*Above*): Public health in London.
The poor water supply and inadequate sewers of early 19th-century cities led to outbreaks of cholera and other diseases. One of the first attempts to deal with this problem in London was the establishment of the Metropolitan Commission of Sewers in 1848. After the commission was replaced by the Metropolitan Board of Works in 1855, a set of its printed records was deposited in the British Library. These plans and elevations are from a proposal for a network of public conveniences submitted to the commission in 1849 by Sir Joseph Bazalgette (1819–91), who was afterwards responsible for the construction of London's sewer system and the building of the Thames Embankment.
[Printed Books, 8776.h.29]

73 (*Right*): Florence Nightingale.
Florence Nightingale (1820–1910), whose papers are in the British Library, was largely responsible for the establishment of the modern nursing profession in Britain and fought unceasingly to improve standards of hygiene in hospitals. In 1860, a school for nurses based on Florence Nightingale's principles was established at St Thomas's Hospital in London using money from a fund established in recognition of her services in the Crimea. These are notes made by her on a group of probationary nurses at the school in 1873. She records that Nurse Bather was 'ill tempered', Nurse Evans 'conceited untrustworthy flirting' and Nurse Upton 'not thorough or trustworthy'. Nurse Robinson was 'best' but Nurse Berryman was 'lazy – w^d not give the children the bedpans. Untruthful – mischievous'.
[Add. MS 47762, f.28]

Miss Lemon's Prob?

Bather — ill tempered

Evans — Conceited untrustworthy
flirting — Sat up with S. Salva
night after Hylo

Upton — not thorough or trustworthy

Robinson — best

Berryman — Lazy — wd not give the
children the bed pan
untruthful — mischievous

Hignett — Nurse Maid very good

Sparkes — very poor creature — Giddy

Miss Air — the mischievous — now in Albert
JWilliams — the good little Nurse
Berryman } the embryo (firw rate sup?
Lee } tale bearers & Malon
of Miss Bourne
untruthful — mischievous
that she did not put the
stimulant

Rosewarne her Nurse Mylo
too

Randale her Night Nurse eccentric
Affectation — ill health but
good

Cross formerly Nurse maid
(not Prob?) now Nurse

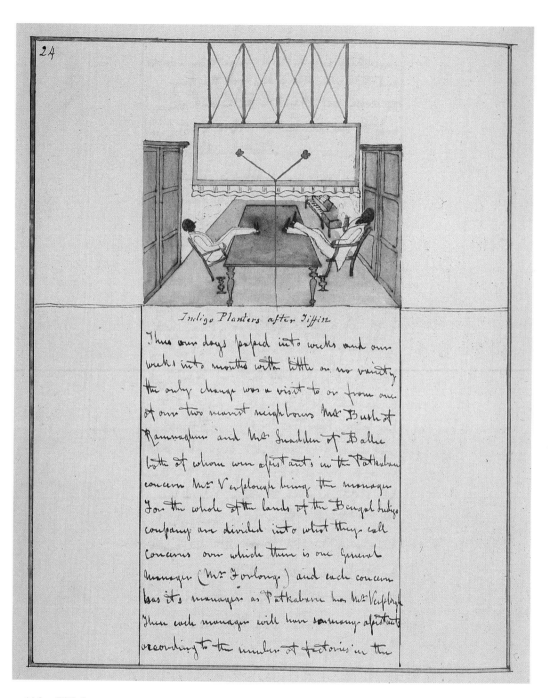

Indigo Planters after Tiffin

74 'After Tiffin'.

Amongst the many documents in the India Office Library depicting the life of English people in India are the journals of Thomas Machell (1824–62), who first travelled to India as a young midshipman after running away from home and later became a plantation manager. This entry describes his quiet life on an indigo plantation.

[India Office Library, MSS EUR B 369, f.142v]

75 The last page of General Gordon's journal.

In 1884 General Charles Gordon single-handedly organised the defence of the Sudanese city of Khartoum, which had only a small garrison of local troops and few supplies, against a siege by rebels which lasted ten months. The town fell and Gordon was killed only two days before the arrival of a relief column. This is the last page of a journal of the siege kept by Gordon on the back of telegraph forms. It ends: 'I have done my best for the honor of our country. Goodbye. C. G. Gordon'. Across the bottom of the page Gordon has scribbled: 'You send me no information though you have lots of money!'.

[Add. MS 34479, f.108]

76 A sketch by Gordon. This sketch by Gordon from an earlier section of his journal comments sardonically on reports that the British High Commissioner in Cairo had been discussing the position at Khartoum with the Egyptian government.

[Add. MS 34479, f.13]

77 A suffragette scrapbook.

This is the cover of a scrapbook compiled by Olive Wharry, recording her activities as a suffragette between 1911 and 1914 while she was a young student. Among the acts of protest in which Olive took part were the burning of the refreshment pavilion in Kew Gardens and the spoiling of mail in letter boxes in Tunbridge Wells. In addition to the prison terms listed by Olive on the cover of her scrapbook, she also spent time in Caernarvon and Liverpool gaols. Olive's scrapbook contains newspaper cuttings relating to incidents in which she was involved, poems and drawings by her and her fellow prisoners and other mementoes of the struggle to secure women the vote.

[Add. MS 49976, f.i]

78 The Stopes papers.
The papers of Dr Marie Stopes (1880–1958) reflect her campaign to encourage greater frankness in sexual matters and increase awareness of birth control methods. This is one of the illustrations from the final draft of her best-selling book, *Married Love*, published in 1918. It shows the level of 'spontaneous desire' in a woman over a period of two months and was intended to illustrate one of Dr Stopes' central themes, that the female sex drive was not as constant as that of a male.
[Add. MS 58506 (unfoliated)]

79, 80 Marie Stopes and birth control.
In 1921, Marie Stopes founded the first birth control clinic in Britain. Illustrated here is a printed slip for doctors and health workers to give patients, advising them of the clinic's work. In order to make advice on birth control available in working class areas and rural districts, Dr Stopes also established mobile clinics in caravans. The photograph shows one such clinic in Bethnal Green in 1928.
[Add. MS 58770 (unfoliated)]
[Add. MS 58601 (unfoliated)]

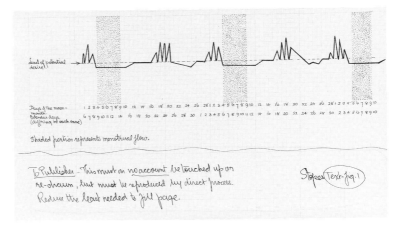

C.B.C.

MOTHERS' CLINIC FOR CONSTRUCTIVE BIRTH CONTROL.

(Originally founded at Holloway, March, 1921. The first Birth Control Clinic in the British Empire.)

Both to spare your own personal distress and to avoid bringing a weakly child into the world, it is important that all should realize that no one should conceive in times of individual misery or ill-health. Of course, wherever a child is already on the way, the best must be made of it. But sound and wholesome methods of Birth Control (Control of Conception) are known and advice will be given free by a qualified nurse to all married persons who present this slip at the

MOTHERS' CLINIC (the First and only FREE Clinic),
108, WHITFIELD STREET, TOTTENHAM COURT ROAD, W.1.

Telephone—MUSEUM 9528.   Open Daily (except Saturdays).
Hours 10 a.m.—6 p.m.

Off Tottenham Court Road, two minutes from Warren Street and Goodge Street Stations.

John Hubert

The Air raid of September 8th

On Wednesday I retired to bed about a quarter past ten. Suddenly I was awakened by the whirring of a propeller and a loud resounding crash mingled with the sound of falling glass. I looked out of my bedroom window to see what was the cause of the disturbance. In the sky I could see a long cigar shaped object, which I at once knew to be a Zeppelin. I ran down to the kitchen where all of our family had assembled. Then we heard the anti-aircraft guns firing at the Zeppelin. We heard about eight shots being fired at it. My brother and I ran to the window again, to see the Zeppelin turning round, the gunfire being so heavy that it it was forced to retreat inland. A bomb had been dropped at the end of Lambs Conduit Passage, and had set fire to the spirit cellar of a public house called the "Dolphin." Also the late "National Penny Bank" was set fire to. The gas main had also caught fire thus making the fire worse than it would have been. Later on my

81 Zeppelin over London. During the First World War, German Zeppelin airships made a number of air raids on Britain. One of the most devastating of these attacks took place on 8 September 1915, when the Zeppelin *L13* dropped about 4,000 pounds of bombs on central London. The area immediately to the east of the British Museum was particularly badly hit. Shortly afterwards, a class of boys at the Princeton Street elementary schools near the Museum wrote essays describing their experiences in the raid, which the headmaster presented to the Library. The beginning of one of the most vivid essays is illustrated here.
[Add. MS 39257, f.2]

82 *The Swiss Cottager.* The British Library contains many examples of magazines published during the Second World War by such local groups as air raid wardens and fire fighters, which vividly evoke life on the 'home front' at this time. The people who regularly took shelter in Swiss Cottage underground station at the height of the bombing of London in 1940 elected a committee to negotiate with the authorities for an improvement in facilities for the shelterers. The committee published a free magazine, *The Swiss Cottager*, a copy of which is shown here.
[Printed Books, PP. 7000.aeg]

P.P.4000.aeg

The Swiss Cottager

De Profundis

Organ of the Air Raid Shelterers at Swiss Cottage Station
London, N.W. 3

BULLETIN No. 2

WE HOPE that our first issue was well-received by all Swiss Cottagers. It has earned wider notice, too, and "The Times," "The Daily Telegraph" (which also had a photograph of it) and "The Daily Express" all praised it. That was very gratifying, for we need all the publicity we can obtain in order to make Tube-shelterers as comfortable as possible.

*   *   *

PENDING the Government's decision on the question of deep-shelters, there is a growing opinion that, as a short-term policy (for, after all, something needs to be done *immediately*) the installation of three-tier bunks on tube platforms would be hailed with relief by the thousands of people who nightly use the tube-station platforms as dormitories, and by the thousands more who, because of lack of space, are prevented from doing so.

*   *   *

THE ADVANTAGES of this are manifold.

Primarily, they would increase the accommodation and so enable more people to have rest and slumber, to say nothing of safety.

They would occupy no more—indeed, less—platform space than is now taken up nightly.

Conditions would be less dangerous to health.

It would more easily enable the station platforms to be kept clean.

They would mean that thousands of Londoners would be enabled to escape the cold and damp of surface-shelters in winter-time.

There would be far less difficulty over the question of reserving places on the platforms. Very likely the problem would no longer exist, for it is conceivable that local users of tube-station shelters might be able to have their regular bunks. There would be equality of comfort for the shelterers.

And the task of the Committee, the station-staff, and the police would be rendered so much easier.

MEANWHILE we are aware of complaints regarding people who reserve places for groups hours before darkness falls and would be very pleased to check this practice, which is unfair to those whose work prevents them from arriving until dusk. But the problem is a difficult one, the more so since any person has the right to enter any tube station as long as it is open. Any practical suggestion will be welcomed and, if possible, acted upon.

Users of deck chairs make our task more difficult, and it is possible that in future they will find themselves stopped by authority from entering the station with them. The Committee's primary aim is *to provide as many sleeping places as possible*. You may be uncomfortable where you lie, but it is blue-pencil more uncomfortable to have to walk about all night for lack of a place to sleep in.

*   *   *

WITH LITTER you are still being far too generous. PLEASE leave the station in the condition in which you find it. It takes but a few seconds for you, but it takes an hour or two of the station-staff's time to make the place presentable most mornings. So will you take your wastepaper, wrappings, cartons, paperbags, etc., away with you?

*   *   *

WATER is now being carried round nightly by the stewards. Please bring your own cups.

*   *   *

TEA: We are seeking facilities from the Board to make tea for you. Thus you could be assured of having it nightly, at an early hour.

P.T.O.

PANDIT NEHRU asked for a further definition of the difference between agreement and acceptance. HIS EXCELLENCY THE VICEROY explained that agreement would imply belief that the right principles were being employed. He had had to violate the principles of both sides, so could not ask for complete agreement. What he asked was for acceptance, in order to denote belief that the plan was a fair and sincere solution for the good of the country. PANDIT NEHRU stated that there could never be complete approval of the plan from Congress, but, on the balance, they accepted it. Mr. NISHTAR pointed out that acceptance of the plan really implied agreement to make it work. HIS EXCELLENCY THE VICEROY agreed with this.

Mr. JINNAH said that it was perfectly true to say that neither side agreed with certain points in the plan. Its formal acceptance by the Muslim League, which would have to come later, and the Constitutional procedure of the League had to be considered. The decision could not be left to the leaders and the Working Committee (of which there were 21 members) alone. There were many important people outside the Working Committee. The leaders and the Working Committee would have to bring the people round. Much explanation would be necessary. Rather than a few representatives of the Muslim League immediately committing themselves, he would rather say that the plan had been fully examined and that they would do their best to see that the proposals were given effect to peacefully and without bloodshed.

HIS EXCELLENCY THE VICEROY said that he was willing to take the risk of accepting the words of the leaders and the backing of their Working Committees. He was completely confident in the loyalty and straightforwardness of the leaders. He would be happy so long as he knew that they were loyally trying to get the Plan accepted. But he had to ask for the preliminary agreement of the Working Committees to support the Plan.

Mr.JINNAH said that he could speak only for himself. He entered into the spirit of the proposals but he would like the Viceroy to consider that, in order to give a definite answer, it was necessary to make the people understand. The Muslim League was a democratic organisation. He and his Working Committee would have to go before their masters, the people, for a final decision.

HIS EXCELLENCY THE VICEROY said that there were times when leaders had to make vital decisions without consulting their followers and trust to carrying them with them at a later stage. In democratic countries, Parliaments could always disagree with the decisions taken by Prime Ministers and by Cabinets. A decision taken at the top and afterwards confirmed by the people would be in accord with democratic processes.

Mr.JINNAH said that, if a ready-made decision was put before the All-India Muslim League Council, which he could convene in a week, they would declare that they had already been committed without having

/been.....

83 Mountbatten and Indian independence.

This is part of the minutes of a momentous meeting held on 2 June 1947 between Lord Mountbatten (1900–1979) as Viceroy of India and the chief Indian political leaders. At this meeting, Mountbatten presented the British government's final proposals for the partition of India and the establishment of independent rule. He asked the Indian leaders to say whether they would help ensure the peaceful implementation of the plan. In the exchanges recorded here, the leaders were seeking clarification of the extent to which Mountbatten wanted them to endorse the proposals. They all finally agreed to accept the plan the following day. As the archives of British rule in India, the India Office Records, of which these minutes are part, are the chief source of information about the British withdrawal from India.

[India Office Records, L/P&J/10/81, f.407]

84 The Falklands war. Popular newspapers can be a useful record of the general mood of the nation in times of crisis. This issue of *The Sun* for 1 May 1982, for example, reflects the jingoistic reaction of many British people to the invasion of the Falkland islands.

[Newspaper Library]

STICK THIS UP YOUR JUNTA!

BATTLE FOR THE ISLANDS

A Sun missile for Galtieri's gauchos

By WENDY HENRY

THE first missile to hit Galtieri's gauchos will come with love from The Sun.

And just in case he doesn't get the message, the weapon will have painted on its side "Up Yours, Galtieri" and will be signed by Tony Snow—our man aboard HMS Invincible.

Argie troops in training in the Falklands

ANDREW INSISTED: I MUST SAIL

Here it comes, senors . . .

COMO EN 1806 Y 1807
HECHEMOS A LOS INGLESES!!
MUERA EL CINISMO YANQUI !!
PAZ CON DIGNIDAD
POR LA VICTORIA:
GOBIERNO DE EMERGENCIA
SIN EXCLUSIONES

PARTIDO COMUNISTA AVELLANEDA-LANUS

LAS MALVINAS
SON
ARGENTINAS

F. A. N. J. PRESENTE

POR DIOS - POR LA PATRIA
HASTA QUE LA MUERTE.
NOS SEPARE DE LA LUCHA

FRENTE DE ACCION NACIONAL JUSTICIALISTA

85, 86 Argentinian handbills.
The Library's collection of foreign literature allows both sides of issues like the Falklands conflict to be readily explored. These two handbills were distributed in Argentina at the time of the war. One declares that the Peronist National Front is ready for action until death separates it from the struggle. The other, issued by the Avellaneda-Lanus communist party, calls for the British to be thrown out as they were when they invaded the Argentinian mainland in 1806 and 1807 and demands the formation of an emergency government in Argentina containing representatives of all parties.

[Printed Books (uncatalogued)]

Suggestions for further reading

The starting point for anyone interested in the materials of English history is the (unfortunately not yet complete) series of *English Historical Documents* published under the general editorship of David C. Douglas by Eyre and Spottiswoode from 1953, which contains a rich collection of extracts from all kinds of sources, translated where necessary, with valuable introductions and bibliographies. Other general collections of historical documents include H. Ellis, *Original letters, illustrative of English history*, London, 1824–36, based almost entirely on the British Library's collections, the series *They Saw It Happen* published under various editors by Basil Blackwell from 1953, A. E. Bland, P. A. Brown and R. H. Tawney, *English Economic History, Selected Documents*, London, 1914, and C. Stephenson and F. G. Marcham, *Sources of English Constitutional History*, New York, 1937. Lively general surveys of the types of English historical documents and problems of interpretation raised by them are J. J. Bagley, *Historical Interpretation*, London, 1971, G. R. Elton, *England, 1200–1640*, Cambridge, 1969, A. Macfarlane, *A Guide to English Historical Records*, Cambridge, 1983 and W. B. Stephens, *Sources for English Local History*, 2nd ed., Cambridge, 1981. The most lucid introduction to the reading of the handwriting in historical documents is L. C. Hector, *The Handwriting of English Documents*, London, 1958. Examples of typical documents with full transcripts are given in H. E. P. Grieve, *Some Examples of English Handwriting*, Essex Record Office, 1949, and *More Examples of English Handwriting*, Essex Record Office, 1950. On problems of dates, the indispensable guides are C. R. Cheney, *Handbook of Dates*, London, 1958, and E. B. Fryde *et al.*, *Handbook of British Chronology*, 3rd ed., 1986. The best short history of England is the *Oxford Illustrated History of England*, ed. K. O. Morgan, Oxford, 1984. Of the literature on the Library's collections, the two books which give the best general overview of the collections, although both now somewhat dated, are J. P. Gilson, *A Student's Guide to the Manuscripts of the British Museum*, S. P. C. K. Helps for Students of History, no. 31, London, 1920, and A. Esdaile, *The British Museum Library*, London, 1946.

87 Photograph of Queen Victoria and her Scots attendant, John Brown, from the album of Jane, Lady Waterpark, one of the queen's ladies-in-waiting.
[Add. MS 60751, f.2]